PETTICOAT PRISONERS

∽ OF OLD WYOMING ∽

OTHER BOOKS BY Larry K. Brown

The Hog Ranches of Wyoming:
    Liquor, Lust, & Lies Under Sagebrush Skies

You Are Respectfully Invited to Attend My Execution

PETTICOAT PRISONERS

∽ OF OLD WYOMING ∽

Larry K. Brown

with a foreword by Nola Blackburn

HIGH PLAINS PRESS

10   9   8   7   6

Library of Congress Cataloging-in-Publication Data

Brown, Larry K.
Petticoat prisoners of Old Wyoming / by Larry K. Brown;
with a foreword by Nola Blackburn.
p. cm.
Includes bibliographical references and index.
ISBN 0-931271-55-X (hardcover) --
ISBN 0-931271-56-8 (paper)
1. Women prisoners--Wyoming--History
2. Female offenders--Wyoming--History
3. Prisons--Wyoming--History.
I. Title.
HV9475.W8 B76 2000
364.3'74'09787--dc21   00-033460

HIGH PLAINS PRESS

539 CASSA ROAD
GLENDO, WYOMING 82213
www.highplainspress.com
Catalog available.
1-800-552-7819

For Florence, my wife;
Marjorie, my mother;
Mary Ellen, my mother-in-law;
Addie and Caroline, my grandmothers;
and all the other women who made and make the West
the most wonderful place in which to live.

. . . three codes of morals [exist] in the old west . . . One for women, one for men and one for royalty. Women must be virtuous or be socially damned; men may do as they please, provided they pay their club bills and do not cheat at cards; royalty— well, there a divinity doth hedge a king who makes of his orgies very proper tea parties. The one sympathetic link in these several codes is that nobody—not even a woman—loses caste unless found out!

KATE FIELDS, PROMINENT WASHINGTON, D.C. JOURNALIST AND PUBLISHER OF "KATE FIELDS'S WASHINGTON"

Untitled news item, Cheyenne Daily Sun, Cheyenne, Wyoming, July 24, 1891

CONTENTS

Foreword

I recall clearly the day Larry Brown first contacted me, requesting specific background information about our inmates that he wished to include in this book, *Petticoat Prisoners of Old Wyoming*. His enthusiasm, his obvious commitment to this subject, and most especially his open and articulate sharing of information about Wyoming's criminal past, appealed to me. Also, he piqued my abiding curiosity about those of my gender—whether heroines or villains—who have contributed to our history.

Unfortunately, however, I was unable to give him some of the data he desired, because many facts about our inmates are confidential and may not be shared with individuals outside our Department of Corrections or the Criminal Justice System. Nonetheless, Larry's outstanding research of materials in the public domain unearthed many unknown facts and enabled him to produce this extraordinary account about Wyoming's earliest female felons.

For example, I learned that an unfortunate soul named "Molly" Wrisinger was the first criminal of her sex to serve time in Wyoming's State Penitentiary when it was located in Laramie. More than a thousand more unfortunates followed in her footsteps. Larry's vivid accounts of the women's crimes, trials, and prison experiences left me feeling, too, that I could almost hear the sounds, smell the odors, feel the atmosphere, see the surroundings, and share the events as they happened. And I was reminded that the colorful stories of such women often have common themes: addiction, co-dependency, greed, lust, mental illness, and criminal thinking. Many also share some of the same character strengths and flaws: extreme independence, dominance, aggression, and, yes, violence. Some were passive, dependent, fearful, and easily dominated. But still others had strong, well-defined egos and identities with the spiritual strength needed to effectively balance their lives.

I found it a bit surprising that, although Larry has not worked in my profession, his writing about it truly brings the subjects to life, while clearly recreating situations and circumstances that I have come to know so well during my twenty-three-plus years of experience as a corrections professional with the Wyoming Women's Center (WWC). I was reminded, for instance, that as wardens we are ordered by judges to keep, govern, and sustain those in our charge even though many of the resources that we need to do those jobs are in short supply. I am especially conscious of this fact as this growth industry moves into the twenty-first century.

Thanks to Larry's account of early penitentiary life, I believe you also will gain some insight into the unusual complexity of our business: staff and inmates doing time together, sharing the prison experience. It is an extremely difficult balance for the "keepers" to assure the "kept" are held safely and securely while providing a sane environment that offers positive opportunities for those inmates who want to change their lives. To see the humanity and evil in people held in custody, yet lawfully treat each with professionalism and bona fide uncorrupted authority, truly requires sharp consciousness at all times.

I particularly was interested in Larry's epilogue, because it traces the evolution of Wyoming's penal system for women from 1909, the year they left the State Penitentiary in Rawlins, where they shared walls with men, until they were returned to our state many years later. In the interim, they were incarcerated at the Colorado State Penitentiary in Cañon City, Colorado, before being sent first to Leavenworth, Kansas, and then back to Cañon City. Still later, they were moved to York, Nebraska. Finally, in June 1976, the five elected officials of the State Board of Charities and Reform learned that Nebraska authorities were seriously considering ejecting Wyoming women from the York facilities. Only six months later, SBCR officials were told the State of Nebraska Department of Correctional Services would "no longer accept Wyoming's women felons after June 3, 1977." Wyoming women prisoners subsequently were returned to our Cowboy State, where they were housed in special quarters at the state hospital in Evanston. And that is when (June 20, 1977) I began my career as a WWC

Corrections Officer, supervised by Judith Uphoff, who now heads the State's Department of Corrections.

Not long thereafter, the need for a permanent and separate corrections facility for women became apparent. Recognizing the problem, the Forty-Fifth Legislature instructed the SBCR to recommend a site for a permanent location. At the general session of the next legislative assembly, State Auditor Jim Griffith moved that Lusk, Wyoming, be selected as the most desirable site, a recommendation promptly seconded and passed. A formal groundbreaking ceremony took place at the Niobrara County seat on August 11, 1982. Two years later, I was assigned to begin staff training at the new penal institution, which opened for business on Saturday, September 8. The following Tuesday, a chartered bus arrived with the rest of our staff and thirty-eight inmates. From that date through December 31, 1999, 758 more women have served time here in Lusk. Regrettably, there is no end in sight.

I'm proud to say that the many investments made by people of Wyoming in this institution, its staff, and its rehabilitative programs have returned big dividends over the years. Our structures are safe, secure, and in excellent condition. The grounds are well maintained. Thanks to professional management and administrative insistence on superior standards, the WWC consistently is touted as one of the finest correctional institutions in America. And, most important, our carefully supervised inmates are serving their sentences according to conditions prescribed by law while, at the same time, our staff and volunteers are helping them prepare to reenter society as useful, productive citizens.

In summary, I feel blessed to have been a pioneer in Wyoming's corrections career field. I also am honored to be one of the first to review Larry K. Brown's *Petticoat Prisoners of Old Wyoming*. I'm certain that as you read his following stories, you, too, will learn much about female felons and gain an even greater appreciation about their difficult lives in old Wyoming.

NOLA BLACKBURN, WARDEN
WYOMING WOMEN'S CENTER, LUSK, WYOMING

Preface

Petticoat Prisoners of Old Wyoming is the third volume of a trilogy about Wyoming's wicked ways. This book begins with the incarceration of the first woman prisoner at the Wyoming Territorial Penitentiary in July 1880 and includes the story of each subsequent female felon imprisoned there and at the State Penitentiaries in Laramie and Rawlins until the release of the last such in-state woman prisoner in September 1909.

My first book — *The Hog Ranches of Wyoming: Liquor, Lust, and Lies Under Sagebrush Skies* — tells the origin and history of "hog ranches." At such rural establishments, a customer might while away his free time with a shot of rye, a game of faro, and a roll in the crib with a "soiled angel" made passably attractive by loneliness and miles of sage. Crimes at those sites also resulted in the first *legal* executions in the Wyoming Territory. Thus, my second book, *"You Are*

Respectfully Invited to Attend My Execution," tells the stories of the seven star-crossed men who were tried, convicted, and legally executed before Wyoming gained statehood. Ironically, Mary [née Marker] Wrisinger, the stepdaughter of the last of those men, subsequently fell afoul the law and became the first woman convicted and imprisoned at the Wyoming State Penitentiary in Laramie.

The individual stories of the twenty-two women who served time in Wyoming's great state pens, however, could not have been told in detail or so effectively without the help of friends who share my curiosity and love of history. Laramie, Wyoming, historian Elnora L. Frye, for example, inspired me to write about Wyoming criminal history. Her research and scholarship, as published in *The Atlas of Wyoming Outlaws at the Territorial Penitentiary*, greatly eased my early efforts in search of such stories.

I wish to thank, too, the Wyoming Territorial Park staff in Laramie for providing details regarding the lives of women imprisoned there at the penitentiary as well as helping me understand the strict prison routine and the inmates' day-to-day lifestyle.

Mark Setright, Executive Director of the Wyoming Frontier Prison at Rawlins, also won my heartfelt thanks for his tireless, professional guidance and help with information and photos not previously published about the prisoners and staff of that institution.

And, I express my appreciation to the Wyoming State Archives staff. Most specifically, the aid and guidance by Curtis Greubel, supervisor of the Wyoming Division of Cultural Resources, and his reference historians—Jean Brainerd,

LaVaughn Bresnahan, Cindy Brown, and Ann Nelson—who brought to light most of the original criminal case files so necessary for developing this book. Photographer Craig Pindell's superlative assistance helped me, too, with the selection and production of pictures to illustrate this volume.

Another historical expert, who generously shared his time, energy, and expertise with me in the production of this book is Rick Ewig, Associate Director for Administration at the University of Wyoming's American Heritage Center in Laramie and Cheyenne, Wyoming.

I thank Nancy Curtis, my publisher, for her friendship. Her unfailing confidence and support continue to encourage my relatively brief but grateful career as a historian and writer of the Old West.

I am indebted, too, to Wyoming Women's Center Warden Nola Blackburn, not only for her insightful and generous foreword to this book, but for a career of caring, as well as her professional service, on behalf of our state's women's correctional programs and activities.

And my wife, Florence, whom I most respect, remains my greatest cheerleader as well as the editorial critic upon whom I most rely.

Lastly, you, the reader, may note that the many quotes in this book are rife with spelling, capitalization, and grammatical errors. We have chosen to keep those miscues in the text true to the original documents, because we believe such blemishes not only help retain the authenticity of the original sources, but help give a sense of those who recorded that information. We hope you agree.

LARRY K. BROWN
CHEYENNE, WYOMING

Introduction

Imagine this. Once high-spirited women shared the same drab and drafty room. Day and night. Cheek by jowl. Only bars and a grid of strap-iron veiled their most intimate moments. They awoke each morning to the harsh, metallic call of a bell. The clang of a clapper, rather than a voice, directed each lock-step during the rest of their strict, cloistered day. Many of the women bathed in cold water from the same bucket . . . lathered with the same bar of lye soap . . . ate the same bland food . . . used the same stained toilet. Neither flagellants nor nuns of a medieval order, these petticoat prisoners, convicted by the courts for committing felonies, suffered imprisonment in the territorial penitentiary and, later, state prisons of old Wyoming for their sins against society.

The Wyoming Territorial Penitentiary in Laramie which was dedicated on July 15, 1872, to "evil Doer's of all Classes and Kinds," accepted the first prisoner on January 13, 1875. After Wyoming became a state on July 10, 1890, authorities redesignated it as the Wyoming State Penitentiary. (American Heritage Center)

Roughly seven and a half years after Wyoming's founding fathers opened the Wyoming Territorial Penitentiary's doors at Laramie City in January 1873 to convicted felons, law enforcement officers arrested and imprisoned NETTIE STEW-ART-WRIGHT there as their first woman inmate. Suspected of stealing arms and ammunition with soldiers Leonard Starr and Louis Blackwood from the U.S. Army at Fort McKinney, Nettie warmed her cell in the pen from the last week of July 1880 until August 6, 1880. Authorities dropped their charges against the trio due to insufficient facts.

Three years later, in June 1883, U.S. Marshal Gustave Schnitger arrested FLORENCE W. HUGHES, a boarding house-keeper in Cummins City, and her friend, John M. Cool-broth, for selling liquor without a license. After paying their bail, they, too, left prison and avoided conviction thanks to a lack of evidence.

Nettie and Florence were never convicted and therefore enjoy unique status. Authorities held them only "for safe-keeping."

Which brings us to JENNIE BERRY and ANNA PETERSON, who fit still another convict category: women sentenced to terms in Wyoming's Territorial penitentiary, but who served their sentences, instead, in their respective county jails. How did that happen?

On March 8, 1882, Wyoming's Board of Penitentiary Commissioners signed a contract with Joliet, Illinois, prison management in which the Illinois prison agreed to accept "free of charge, except for transportation," all Wyoming prisoners sentenced to six months or more. That arrangement not only helped solve Wyoming's growing penal problem, but provided Illinois with an increased pool of convict labor.

That system seemed to work well until the contract expired five years later. When Illinois officials refused to renew the deal, Wyoming's Penitentiary Commissioners apparently felt compelled to resolve their problem for prison space by designating county jails as "territorial penitentiaries" and the sheriffs of those facilities as wardens of the territorial prisoners for the year 1887. Which takes us to the cases involving Jennie and Anna.

On June 13, 1887, officials locked up Jennie Berry and three cohorts in crime—Aderan (aka Edward) Everett, Robert Sanderson, and David Lewis—in the Wyoming Territorial Penitentiary. Later authorities individually charged members of the "Fort Laramie Quartette," as the newspapers referred to their group, with the murder of Richard Rice, a settler who lived some twelve miles east of Fort Laramie on the North Platte River.

It seems, while traveling through the area three months earlier, Jennie left her husband for a life with Rice. Within only hours, however, she changed her mind and moved in with Everett, who sometimes shared his cabin a mile or so further east along the river with Sanderson and Lewis. When Rice went to retrieve his lover on March 11, Everett and Sanderson shot and killed the distraught suitor, then threw his body in the river.

After searchers found Rice's corpse the following October 5 on a sandbar, the court tried and released Lewis, but convicted Everett and Sanderson for manslaughter and sentenced each to four years at the Joliet Penitentiary in Illinois. For her role as an "Accessory After the Fact," William L. Maginnis, Chief Justice of the Wyoming Territory's Supreme Court and presiding First Judicial District Court Judge, fined Jennie Berry two hundred dollars and sentenced her to two years in the Laramie County Jail in Cheyenne.

Anna Peterson, the mother of three children, suffered a similar fate, but for a quite different crime. The forty-four year-old and her husband, Louis, were held in the Fremont

County Jail from November 11, 1887, until July 16, 1888, when they were tried in the Third Judicial District Court for stealing "One head of neat cattle [a common, domestic bovine] of the value of Twenty five Dollars of the goods and chattels of One John McLaughlin." Although the jury found Louis not guilty and ordered him immediately released, Anna would share no such luck. Instead, the court determined the critter to be worth but sixteen dollars, but the jury still found Anna guilty as charged, and the judge sent her back to her cell to serve six months and pay a fine of three hundred dollars, plus court costs.

Although family and friends launched a massive letter writing campaign to Governor Thomas Moonlight in hope of gaining Anna's early release, their efforts just delayed matters while their petitions snailed their way through the bureaucracy, then languished on the Chief Executive's desk as he struggled with his decision. Consequently, it was not until November 10, 1888—nearly four months after her sentencing—that the good Governor pardoned her and released her from jail so that she could return to her family.

After Wyoming joined the Union on July 10, 1890, as its forty-fourth state, jurors convicted twenty more women of felonious, or serious, crimes against society. Found guilty of such offenses, each of those inmates received a number to identify her as a bona fide incarcerated felon and testifying to her infamy as a "guest" of Wyoming's infamous "Gray Bar Hotel."

Wyoming's First "Numbered" Female Felons

SATURDAY AFTERNOON excitement filled the air of old Laramie City as hundreds of eager folk poured through the canvas flap and into the sun-warmed tent to see the 1891 Adam Forespaugh Shows: the "greatest tented exhibition in the world."

The din of the crowd, as well as the heady smell of fresh hay and animal odors, only added to the aura. In fact, those sensory delights, plus the spangled tights and colored lights, dazzled almost everybody but Cassius and Eva Webber. The familiar, rather than the unusual, apparently caught the couple's eyes. A fur-trimmed jacket attracted their attention. And they noticed it because when last they'd seen it, it had been safely hanging in their closet at home. Now Eva's treasured jacket was being worn by a woman unknown to them!

For those of you who may be considering crime as a vocation, please heed this bit of friendly advice. If you ever steal clothing, never wear the pilfered garment in public, particularly if you live in a relatively small town like Laramie. Regrettably, "Mollie" (Mary Sophia née Marker) Wrisinger and Belle Jones learned that lesson too late. Constable Harry Tatham immediately responded to the Webbers' call for help and, after identifying the well-feathered "soiled doves," he arrested them and took them to the local jail for questioning. Although Mollie and Belle claimed "dress maker" and "nurse" as their respective professions, men about town knew them better as prostitutes.

Based upon a tentative identification of the garments, the Webbers filed an official complaint with J.H. Hayford, Justice of the Peace. The justice, in turn, issued a warrant to search a well-known brothel, where the two women lived, on the west side of the Laramie River. Later that day, authorities found in the defendants' home articles matching the descriptions of those reported as stolen on or about July 30 from the Webbers' home. In addition to the "ladies jacket trimmed with fur ($3.00)," authorities found a variety of other items, including shoes, a silver plate, "two Christmas cards ($1.00)... one book entitled 'Light of the Nations' ($3.00)... one cuspidor ($0.25)" and a "shaving mug ($0.50)." The Webbers estimated the total value of their losses at $81.25. Mollie and Belle, in turn, protested their innocence by claiming they "purchased the goods from a tramp."

Unconvinced by such arguments in the face of damaging evidence and testimony by witnesses at the August 24 hearing, Justice Hayford ordered the pair to be held on bonds of $250 each to answer grand larceny charges at the forthcoming term of the Second Judicial District Court. Mollie, however, had only $13.85 in her possession at the time of her arrest while Belle apparently had no money. Because neither produced the required bail, the judge found them "in default" and immediately jailed the pair.

In a separate legal action that day, Edward W. Lake filed a complaint against Mollie and Belle for "petit larceny." According to his allegations, he suspected them of "unlawfully purloining some wearing apparel from his tent." Following sworn testimony by witnesses Lake, his wife Nellie, and others, Justice Hayford not only found the defendants guilty of the crimes as charged, but he immediately ordered them "confined in the county jail for the term of the twenty days each."

Except for bad luck, Mollie and Belle had none because, four days later, the home they rented caught fire about three-thirty in the afternoon. According to a local newspaper report:

> The fire department made a hasty run and found the fire had caught from the kitchen chimney and extended under the entire roof of the building. Holes were cut in the room and the flames extinguished. A hole was burned through the west end of the kitchen.

Another sad sidebar to this story involved Belle's six unattended children. Constable Tatham arrested Belle's eldest child, fifteen-year-old "Ella" [Ellen M.] on September 8, when, left to her own devices, the lass committed an unspecified charge of juvenile delinquency. Whatever the crime, its seriousness caused Judge J.W. Blake of the District Court to sentence her to four years at the Good Shepherd Industrial School in Denver, Colorado. Less than two weeks later (September 19), the Albany Board of County Commissioners directed Sheriff Charles Yund to round up the rest of Belle's brood as "indigent" children and take them to join Belle's mother, a patient at the Good Shepherd's Home for the elderly in Denver. After picking up the five younger ones on September 21, the sheriff delivered Ellen and her siblings to their respective institutions two days later.

Mollie, too, had a child, but, in her absence, it is believed her family took in the youngster.

A CASE FOR CONVICTION

By the time the district court convened at ten the morning of September 18 to try Mollie and Belle for the Webbers' charges, overwhelming evidence had mounted against the defendants. In fact, the trial proved merely a formality. After listening to the testimony for only one day, the jurors returned the next morning to declare, "We the jury . . . find each of the defendants guilty as charged." The district court judge then sentenced defendants Mollie and Belle to eighteen months each in the grim Wyoming State Penitentiary, but they did not report immediately to that institution, because of delayed construction of the "female department."

Two days later, however, Sheriff Yund loaded his prisoners aboard a horse-drawn wagon and drove across a small bridge west of town that spanned the bright waters of the river from which the city of Laramie takes its name. A rough dirt road led them to a deep-set door, reinforced with iron, on the west side of the prison. There, the lawman rang the bell at the entrance which, like the windows that frame it, are trimmed in red sandstone. A few moments later, they heard a bold brass key enter the lock before the great door swung silently back into the darkness, on huge hand-forged hinges. After they passed through the two-foot-thick wall of hand-quarried limestone, a guard locked the door behind them before returning the key to its hook on a board. Loaded revolvers and Winchester rifles stood at attention in a large gun case on the wall. In the soft filtered light and cool shade of the pen's gray walls, the trio passed down the short corridor and turned right before making a quick left into a small room, where an administrator interviewed the women and recorded their descriptions.

MOLLIE WRISINGER, #10

Although more than eleven hundred male prisoners had preceded Mollie into that prison since the first convict entered there in January 1873, she had the distinction of being designated convict #10, the first "numbered" woman prisoner to be jailed there. According to her penitentiary admittance record, the petite prisoner weighed only ninety-seven pounds and stood but five-foot, one-half-inch tall. Framed by light brown hair, her broad face and high cheekbones complemented a fair complexion and eyes that seemed to change with the light from gray to blue. Mollie claimed her age as twenty-six, having been born in California in approximately 1865, and that her family raised her in the Baptist faith. Those aware of her past knew her husband James C. Wrisinger left her when she chose to testify against her stepfather George A. Black, whom the State of Wyoming had tried, convicted, and executed for murdering a hermit on Pole Mountain northeast of Laramie.

BELLE JONES, PRISONER #11

The lawmen next logged Mollie's thirty-three-year-old cohort in crime, Belle Jones, as "Prisoner #11." At 145 pounds, the five-foot, six-inch tall brunette, with a dark complexion and deep blue-black eyes, in no way physically resembled her friend. But similarities existed: the Massachusetts-born madam also professed the Baptist faith. Like Molly's husband, Belle's spouse—Edward F. Jones—also had deserted his family. According to acquaintances, he caught "gold fever" in February 1889 and went to Alaska.

Following their in-processing, a guard led the prisoners through the hall to another strong door, where a second key admitted them to the south wing of the prison, one of two such three-tiered cellblocks in which prisoners lived. Through an opening in the thick wall, the cellhouse keeper passed the key back to the "rounder" (guard). He, in turn, led the women through his section, while an armed sentry watched their every move from his cage perched high above the stone floor. With his weapon cocked and primed, the lookout stood poised to pour down death should the new prisoners pose a threat. It took but a few minutes before the small group marched up the stairs to the "female department," an airy, sun-drenched room on the second floor in the southwest corner of the prison. There, Mollie and Belle found meager furnishings, including two crude beds with straw-filled mattresses and nightstands to hold a few of their personal belongings. Prison officials also provided them with chamber pots as well as a pair of chairs and a table.

In the coming days, Mollie and Belle slowly adjusted to the prison's strict monastic regimen. Promptly at 5:30 A.M. on Monday through Saturday, six taps of a bell awoke the inmates and directed them to clean their cells. Half an hour later, the bell rang twice, calling them to breakfast. They knew instinctively that when they heard the clapper strike three times at seven A.M. they must report for work. Two rings at noon meant dinner and, if they behaved well, some rest or exercise. An hour later, the incessant bell rang three times more, returning them to their labors, only to chime again at six P.M. for supper and one hour later to end the treasured rest or recreation period.

Sundays seemed hardly different, with the exception that prisoners might enjoy thirty additional minutes' sleep and have an additional half hour to clean their cells. The remainder of each Sabbath remained work free.

THE "DARK CELL"

Mollie did not do well in adjusting to the rules of the prison. Although her conduct is described in official records as "fair," it did not start that way. Less than three weeks after her admittance, guard George H. Chapman reported that, despite his orders, she refused to "keep quiet." The newly assigned Warden George Briggs, however, apparently got Mollie's attention by having her locked away in the dreaded "dark cell." The enclosure, although the same size as the others in the block, could be sealed from light simply by closing the small, eye-level, sheet-iron port through which a guard could pass bread and water. For violating the strict rules governing prisoner communications, they confined her there for twenty-five consecutive hours—in the dark and without contact with other prisoners—until seven A.M. the following day. Although the violation is the only offense officially recorded against Mollie, she established her unsavory reputation quickly and permanently. At the first Sunday religious service conducted at the penitentiary, for example, Mollie and Belle joined the forty other inmates, who sat on benches along the west wall of the second-floor hall that doubled as a chapel. Because of her bad attitude, a senior guard ordered one of his underlings "to yank her out if she made a bad break." Apparently, she failed to behave, because officials allegedly barred her from attending any future religious services there.

Belle, it seems, fared better. Her behavior during her incarceration is described as "good" by prison authorities.

Following Mollie's rough introduction to prison life, she and Belle apparently adapted to the system and quietly served out the rest of their sentences. This is evidenced by the fact the State Board of Charities and Reform rewarded the behavior of each woman with "five (5) days good time," a five-dollar cash gratuity, and clothing valued at fifteen dollars prior to their release from prison on March 15, 1893. They and fellow prisoner Tom Morrisey (Prisoner #86, grand larceny)—with whom they entered prison—became the first inmates released under a law passed that year by the state legislature that granted allowances for "good time" served.

Favoring anonymity, they eased back into society and faded quickly into obscurity. Their only legacy of note is their infamy as the "first ladies" of the Wyoming State Penitentiary.

Sources Cited

The following types of primary source materials, unless described otherwise, are kept at the Wyoming State Archives in Cheyenne, Wyoming: city directories, microfilmed newspapers, territorial and state census information, justice of the peace records, city jail registers, county criminal District Court cases, State Board of Charities and Reform minutes and correspondence, petitions for pardons, state penitentiary records—including individual convict admittance, disciplinary, and release files—and Supreme Court case decisions, plus supporting documents and correspondence.

For details regarding the lives and crimes of Mollie Wrisinger and Belle Jones, interested parties may find such information in Albany County District Court Criminal Case File #533. Individual Wyoming State Penitentiary Prisoner files for Prisoner #10 and Prisoner #11, which contain the women's respective admittance and release information, offer invaluable supplementary facts about their histories. Related minutiae, as well as the public's perception of and reaction to those women and their crimes, are in such newspaper accounts as those found in the *Laramie Weekly Sentinel*, the *Laramie Boomerang*, and the *Cheyenne Daily Leader* for the period of August 22, 1891, through November 30, 1891.

Additional personal information about Mollie and Belle is contained in Albany County Marriage Records (Roll #4-5, August 8, 1880, January 28, 1883); the

Laramie, Wyoming, Police Docket (January 23, 1891, pp. 59, 70, and 73); Albany County Register of Prisoners (Prisoners #222 and #223, 1891, pp. 86-87); the Albany County Justice of the Peace Docket (August 24, 1891, p. 22); and Wyoming State Board of Charities records. Also, information about Mollie's family may be found in the Wyoming Territorial Census for Albany County (Rock Creek Village, Supervisor's District #1, Enumeration District #22, June 3, 1880, p. 4). A chilling account of prisoner rule infractions and punishments is included in the Wyoming State Penitentiary Prisoner Disciplinary Record (State Government Charities and Reforms, May 1892-October 1906). Still another important document, that may be found in Governor DeForest Richard's official records (Box 3) at the archives, is the "Monograph of the State Penitentiary," written by F.C. Schuckers, Prisoner #410, for presentation at the International Congress of 1900 at Brussels, Belgium. Written for Warden Norman D. McDonald, the October 10, 1899, treatise provides great insight into the prisoners' lives and penitentiary's procedures.

Without question the most valuable secondary sources of material about these women include Elnora L. Frye's *Atlas of Wyoming Outlaws at the Territorial Penitentiary* (Laramie, Wyoming: Jelm Mountain Publications, 1990) and her research-enriched letters to the author. The *Wyoming Territorial Park Visitor's Guide* also provides important information about the history of that institution as well as the "female department" (later called the "women's ward").

Another valuable bit of information that explains the hourly regimentation and control of prisoners is contained in a document entitled "Prison Hours"; the U.S. Department of Justice document may be found in the files of the National Archives in Washington, D.C.

The Bob-Tailed Gal

LIKE THE MAN AND his pals who hiked the mountains and met an angry bear, he cared not if he could outrun the beast. It mattered only that he be faster than his friends.

Unfortunately, Alice Pleasants shared that dilemma one chilly, December 9 morn in 1891. As she and two white "clients" strolled Cheyenne's infamous "Bob-Tail District," the trio met Alice's dusky roommate-competitor Florence Gaines and pimp Isaac Marshall. That is when tempers flared and the "johns" fled, leaving Alice to face fate on her own. Accusing the dark-skinned Alice of "interference" with potential customers, nineteen-year-old Florence pulled a gun and fired. When she missed her target, Isaac grabbed Alice's left arm and passed a large knife to tiny Florence, who "made mince meat of the Pleasants woman." Three times, the sharp blade found its mark as Alice begged for her life, but, according to a newspaper report of the incident, "her supplications were of no avail." Despite Isaac's grip, made strong by his job of molding bricks, Alice broke free, but fell heavily as she started to run down the street. Florence again pounced on Alice and stabbed her three more times. As the victim shrieked with pain, Isaac and Florence fled down an alley and disappeared toward Crow Creek.

Attracted by the gunshot and the women's cries, police raced to the scene. Within hours, the lawmen chased Florence and Isaac to ground, before imprisoning and charging the couple with "purposely, maliciously and feloniously [trying] to kill and murder." In the meantime, bystanders took Alice to nearby (A.E.) Roedel's drug store for treatment by Dr. J.J. Marston. Although she lost much blood from the most serious wounds, she recovered and returned to the streets several days later.

THEIR DAY IN COURT

With officials of the District Court of the First Judicial District already in session in Cheyenne, justice moved swiftly.

When Isaac's attorney successfully filed a motion for a separate trial on the grounds that his client's case might be unfairly tainted by Florence's brutality, Judge Richard H. Scott immediately brought Florence's case before the court. One week later, after the jury heard the victim and other witnesses describe their versions of the deadly assault, the jury adjourned to study the evidence. Within hours, they reached their verdict: "We the jury . . . do find the defendant Florence Gains guilty [of] assault with the intent to kill."

This unusual photo of prisoners in a Denver, Colorado, jail cell appears to have been staged. (Denver Public Library Western History Department)

Twenty-six-year-old Isaac, arraigned as an accessory to the crime, next came before the court. Later that evening, the jurors retired to a separate room before, again, they reached a consensus: "Guilty... as charged," but with the recommendation that he be given "the mercy of the court."

The following Sunday, Florence and Isaac returned to Judge Scott's bench for sentencing, where he ruled that Florence receive two years "at hard labor" in the State Penitentiary at Laramie. To those who witnessed the trial, Florence seemed to accept her fate with little emotion . . . that is, until Isaac stood and faced the court. Practically prostrating himself before the judge, Isaac swore himself "an innocent man who had been accidentally drawn into this trouble, but hadn't done 'nawthin.'" While he related his tale of woe, Florence anxiously watched the judge to gauge his reaction. According to witnesses, she seemed to feel betrayed and ready to burst into tears until the court set all doubts at rest by ordering that Isaac join Florence at the pen for a term of eighteen months. Then, according to a news story, "her face brightened up as though she enjoyed the sentence very much." But Isaac, according to the report, did not mirror her joy.

Although they spent their Christmas holiday in Cheyenne's jail, authorities escorted Florence and Isaac four days later to the state pen, where, enrolled as Prisoners #40 and #41, they ushered in the new year, 1892. There, they remained until Isaac, who suffered from syphilitic rheumatism, gained Acting Governor Amos W. Barber's sympathetic pardon on July 11. His discharge came two days later. Florence, the only woman convict during that time, however, did not find freedom until expiration of her sentence on November 6, 1893.

Sources Cited

Laramie County Criminal Case File #3-342 contains the principal primary documents used to develop this story. Other vital research materials at the Wyoming State Archives included the Wyoming State Penitentiary admittance and release records concerning Convict #40 (Florence Gaines) and Convict #41 (Isaac Marshall), as well as documentation regarding Marshall's Petition for Pardon.

Included among the most important vintage newspaper accounts about Florence's crimes and trial are those contained in the *Cheyenne Daily Leader* and the *Daily Sun* for December 8-17, 1891. The 1902 Cheyenne City Directory also proved helpful in establishing various business addresses and ownership for that period.

The Brass Lock Service Mystery

ONLY THE PURR OF WIND through the pines and the call of a wandering bird seemed in 1893 to break the dull days at Miner's Delight. Saturday nights, too, usually proved no more lively. In fact, a visitor to the southeastern tip of the Wind River Range would find in that once-booming gold camp only a handful of miners and men of mixed skills, who spent their lonely hours in decaying log cabins and false-fronted frame stores. Only the arrival of the Rawlins and Northwestern Stage (Lander-Rawlins stage-line) once every three weeks broke the monotony.

James "Jimminy" Kime, postmaster there since 1872, probably rejoiced at the coach's arrival, because he looked forward to sorting the mail and distributing packages. Like most of those who worked for the U.S. Postal Service, Kime took great pride in the speed, efficiency, and security with which mail moved through the system. And well he should. Even a person who lived in that relatively remote part of Wyoming might order merchandise from Omaha, Nebraska, and expect—with confidence—delivery of such goods within five days of the firm's receipt of that order.

Based on such experience, Kime dropped a package containing eight registered letters into the "through" pouch to Rawlins. Postal officials called it their "brass lock service" and only officials at the ends of the stageline possessed keys for such containers. When Kime's pouch reached its destination about 120 miles to the southeast, however, Postmaster Perry L. Smith located the required list of registered items, but found that someone had cut the pouch and stolen the letters. You can imagine the embarrassment and professional concern Kime must have felt when Smith wrote back that the valuables were "not received." Postal authorities immediately launched an investigation.

During the previous two years, similar complaints had come from every postmaster along a triangular route formed by stagestops at Lander (north), South Pass City (south), and the Myersville station (east) near the bridge over the Sweetwater River. During that time, more than two thousand dollars in currency and property turned up missing. The losses included such improbable items as a photograph, a pair of ladies' gloves, a book, a man's tie, and a dozen handkerchiefs. More valuable items also disappeared: cash, a knife, and a lady's wrap. The vandalized pouch and theft of registered mail, however, offered the first solid evidence that might be used to break the case.

THE INVESTIGATION BEGINS

U.S. Postal Inspector C.M. Waters, assigned to look into the matter, began by writing to the eight addressees, advising them of the most recent theft. He found himself more than a little perplexed, however, to learn that although the items disappeared from Kime's pouch, six of the addressees received their letters via regular postal service. And each of those envelopes contained non-negotiable checks, post office orders, or drafts. But the remaining two registered letters, which contained cash, never resurfaced. Fortunately, Miss Jenette "Etta" Zimmerman of Denver, Colorado—one of the six addressees—kept the envelope in which she received checks totaling sixty-five dollars, money sent to her from her brother George A. Zimmerman, of Atlantic City, Wyoming. Although Etta did not recognize the fine, precise hand that addressed her envelope, the writing seemed vaguely familiar to Inspector Waters.

Like a bloodhound, the good inspector Waters retraced the mail's track along the triangular stage route, a junction through which the two main lines of the service converged at Myersville. One daily route went north to Lander. A second route went south from Brownsville to Lewiston and Miner's Delight then on to South Pass City, where a driver picked up the registered mail pouch and carried it back to Myersville for follow-on delivery to Rawlins. Further investigation proved repeatedly that someone, somewhere along that line, repeatedly tampered with the valuable shipments. And each time Inspector Waters reviewed the route, the scent always seemed strongest at the Myersville station, managed by Postmaster John C. Gatlin and his wife, Stella.

When Waters confronted the handsome Stella with Zimmerman's envelope, she readily acknowledged the writing as hers. She explained, however, a stranger on horseback brought the six letters to her home and asked that she address them for him. "Shortly after the stage came in with the mail from the north that day," she said, "a man ... dressed with a wolf-skin cap and in heavy clothing, a man of about medium height, and thirty-five or forty years of age, and having the appearance of a sheep-herder or freighter, came to the Post Office with several letters to be mailed on that day." She recalled one addressee to be "a person by the name of Zimmerman living at Denver." She complied, she said, because she saw nothing wrong with the request. Despite those questionable circumstances, Waters seemed charmed by "the little woman at the bridge" and reported the office as being "honorably managed."

THE THEFTS CONTINUE

But problems persisted as additional valuables disappeared from the mail. Mrs. Robert Dixon, for example, ordered twenty-nine yards of gingham and silk, plus some dress lining, lace, and silk thread, on March 15, 1893, from the Morse Dry Goods Company of Omaha, Nebraska. A few days later, she received a postcard from the company acknowledging receipt of her order and reporting they had shipped her merchandise on March 20. When, after waiting nine more days, the materials failed to arrive, she filed a complaint with Inspector Waters. Others experienced similar disappointments. Many others. For example, Mrs. Hugo Miller at Myersville did not receive the book sent to her from a Chicago store. And a knife, ordered from Vermont by Albert Nelson of South Pass City, Wyoming, never made it there. Twelve handkerchiefs, two neckties, and a pair of gloves sent from Chicago to Seddon Jones in Atlantic City, Wyoming, also failed to complete their journey. A $2.25 lady's wrap, too, never materialized after Mrs. Fred Chamberline in Lewiston, Wyoming, ordered it from a Salt Lake City dry-goods firm.

During the next two months, Inspector Waters and his associate L. Nichols traced every available clue. When, again, the trail led suspiciously to Myersville and the "bewitching" Mrs. Gatlin, the two postal inspectors decided to bait a trap.

They collaborated with William Brown in Brownsville, who mailed a registered letter containing twenty-three dollars to a man in Rawlins. They also included the stage driver in their plan, and, after he dropped the item off at the Myersville post office, he said he saw the Gatlins take the letter into a private room.

When the coach arrived at Rawlins later that day without Brown's registered letter, the detectives filed a complaint with Edmund J. Churchill, Commissioner of the U.S. Circuit Court, calling for the Gatlins' arrest and their indictment for theft of government mail. That same day (April 4) U.S. Marshal J.P. Rankin and his deputy Charles Yund arrested the couple at their home, where a search uncovered "a vast number of valuable articles, some positively identified as having been lost in the mails." Inspector Waters found in the Gatlins' bureau, for example, "a work on Greek mythology, adorned by pencil marks and made valuable by marginal notes in Stella's chirography [penmanship]." It was the same book ordered, but not received, by Mrs. Miller.

He found, too, Mrs. Dixon's entire order of missing dry goods: fourteen yards of apron gingham, ten yards of dress gingham, two yards of China silk, three yards of satin finish dress lining, seven yards of three-inch-wide black lace, and a spool of white sewing silk. Incredibly and unsuccessfully, Stella Gatlin, who took pride in her sewing skills, moaned, "I hope you are not going to take all the goods not made up." When asked how the dress materials came into her possession, Stella said only that she had some of the items for so long she forgot from whence they came. Later, she testified "the goods came in the [Miner's Delight] pouch without wrapping of any kind. There was nothing by which their ownership could be determined, so she laid them aside to await someone's claiming them." The clerk who filled the fabrics order, however, swore she wrapped the bundle in "stout express paper and the best of hardware twine."

In an incident involving the theft of a photograph, Mrs. Zimmerman, stung at least twice by Stella's service, claimed that after sitting for the portrait in Denver she ordered a dozen copies of the print. When only eleven photos arrived in a "securely wrapped and tied" packet, she ordered another copy from the photographer. Some time later, while awaiting the stage's arrival at the Myersville station, a startled Mrs. Zimmerman discovered her missing photo while browsing the Gatlins' album. When confronted, Stella claimed she found the photo loose in an old mail pouch.

After Marshal Rankin and his deputy escorted the Gatlins to Laramie City, authorities charged the couple on May 10 with three indictments—containing eighteen counts—of mail theft. While Stella remained in the Albany County Jail, her husband obtained his release by posting the required seven hundred dollars in bail bonds so he could seek legal counsel and prepare their defense. Lawmen, in the meantime, transferred his spouse to the Laramie County Jail in Cheyenne, where she remained until mid-July when she, too, gained temporary freedom through bail.

STELLA'S STORY

The following Monday, the media reported that Mrs. Gatlin's attorneys, M.C. Brown and C.P. Arnold, submitted to the United States court "One of the most remarkable affidavits ever filed in this state." According to a newspaper story, the document "was couched in the beautiful language . . . and makes good reading in spite of the many legal forms and phrases." The defense team filed the deposition to gain a continuance of their case until the November term of court. In short, the affidavit set forth that Mrs. Gatlin suffered from kleptomania and "that any stealing she may have been guilty of at [the] Myersville post office was the result of a diseased mind." According to a reporter in Cheyenne, "This was the first time that plea [kleptomania] has ever been made in this state and it will be watched with deep interest." The affidavit also included a summary of her history:

> She was born in the city of Syracuse, New York (in 1850), and her mother died when she was three years

old. Her father lived a worthless life and gave her no care or training as a child. At an early time in her life she remembers of being controlled by an ungovernable impulse to take and carry away any worthless and useless thing that might be found lying about and which belonged to other people.

She states that James C. Jones of Syracuse, New York was a school mate of hers and if present in court would swear that at the age of seventeen she was subject to sever pains in the head. He would swear that during these periods she took things from all her schoolmates and that this propensity was a common report among her schoolmates.

She further states that she was heir to an independent fortune, a portion of which was squandered by her father. Afterwards her uncle was made her guardian and she soon learned that he also was squandering her money. As soon as she became of age she took her money and she hastily married and moved to Aurora, Ill., where she became intimately acquainted with a lady named Mary Hess.

If Mrs. Hess was in court she would swear that Mrs. Gatlin was constantly taking trinkets, such as scissors, knives and handkerchiefs with cat like stealth while calling upon her neighbors. No one realized her crimes until the things were found in her room afterward. Then she would not remember where she got them or had no recollection about them. Mrs. Hess would be able to testify that secrecy was a characteristic of her mania, especially did she keep her kleptomania from her husband.

He began to mistreat and abuse her about this time and she returned to Chicago and secured a divorce from him and coming to Wyoming, married John C. Gatlin.

She also speaks of Charles Ward of Troy, New York, who knew her in school and who would be able to prove that as a school scholar she was given to taking things that did not belong to her. There were other witnesses who would swear as to her diseased mind who could be produced if the trial of the case was postponed.

The affidavit also declared it pained her to make such disclosures, because she struggled for years to overcome her illness while keeping the mania a secret from her husband. When John learned her secret, he apparently tried saving Stella from the shame of conviction by pleading guilty to her crimes. Although their attorneys refused to cooperate in the deception, they declared their clients as indigents while gaining a continuance of their case.

In the following months, Stella kept busy "in the millinery business in Cheyenne . . . [and] made herself many friends." With respect to the trial, however, the Gatlins and their attorneys failed to find witnesses to aid their defense.

THE COURT CONVENES AND CONVICTS

The Federal District Court finally reconvened on November 18. From ten A.M., the jury weighed the evidence of the first two of five charges until early evening when, unable to arrive at a verdict, U.S. Attorney Fowler decided to drop the initial charge against John. The barrister chose instead to press his case against Stella.

Finally that evening he concluded his arguments and members of the jury filed out of the courtroom to decide her fate. By midnight, however, unable to agree on a verdict, the jurors retired to the InterOcean Hotel, where they spent the night. Finally, after forty-two hours of intense discussion and disputed evidence on the first two charges, the jurors conceded they could not reach a consensus regarding Stella. They did bring in a verdict of "not guilty" against John, a co-defendant in the joint indictment.

During the second trial that followed (November 23), the focus turned towards two contentious counts contained in the second indictment: the alleged thefts of dry goods sent to Mrs. Dixon and the photograph sent to Mrs. Zimmerman. On November 24 at 9:15 P.M., the jury once more left the courtroom. Returning shortly after midnight, the jurors announced they reached their verdict only after thirteen ballots. During each of the first twelve votes, eleven jurors called for conviction and one for acquittal. They unanimously voted on the thirteenth ballot for conviction. They found Stella guilty of stealing the package sent from the Morse Dry Goods Company, but not guilty on the count relating to the photo. According to the *Cheyenne Daily Sun* reporter, who witnessed the dramatic event:

> A trying scene was enacted in the U.S. Court this morning. It was dramatic in the extreme and the spectators were all visibly affected. Before a righteous judge stood a frail little woman with a pale face and immovable features. She listened intently to the words as they slowly, but distinctly, fell from the lips of his honor.

Back of her sat her husband with his eyes filling with tears and his mouth twitching with emotions.

"Judge Brown," said Judge [John A. Riner] to the senior counsel for Mrs. Stella Gatlin, "I am disposed to dispose of this case against Stella Gatlin at this time. Is there anything that you can suggest to the court?"

Brown said, "I do not know that I can say anything. I know that the court will be as lenient as possible. The person convicted is a woman. Her husband is poor and for that reason was unable to secure witnesses that might have led to her acquittal. I believe that a light punishment will have as good an effect as a heavy one."

"Have you anything to offer?" asked the judge of Mr. Fowler.

"Nothing, your honor," was the reply.

"Mrs. Gatlin, will you stand up," said Judge Riner to the convicted woman, and she arose and stepped up to the bench. "Is there anything you wish to say why judgment should not be passed upon you at this time?" was asked of her.

"I have nothing to say."

"Very well, it becomes my duty to pass judgement upon you in conformity with the verdict of the jury. It is not a pleasant task I am about to perform, I can assure you. The jury could not do anything else than they did under the evidence in the case. You have been plainly proven guilty. Your husband has proven himself to be a man in every sense of the word and has been found not guilty. He has stood by you all through this trouble and has seen to it that you have had as able counsel as can be found in the state. You have had a fair trial and I hope this will be the last time I will ever have to pass judgement on you as a criminal. The judgement of the court is that you be confined in the state penitentiary at Laramie for the period of one year and three months at hard labor. You may be seated."

In silence, and without visible emotion, Stella turned and took her seat. Her actions offered a chilling contrast to those of John, her husband, who appeared nervously distraught. Their attorneys later described the scene as "one of the most dramatic ever witnessed in a court room in the state."

Two days later, Marshal Rankin escorted the "nicely dressed" Stella with her "stoical mein" via rail to Laramie, where she registered as Prisoner #150, the first woman to be imprisoned there after being convicted of committing a federal crime in Wyoming. During an ensuing examination that destroyed the last vestige of her maidenly modesty, a processing clerk noted her "Weight: 108#; Features regular; large eyes; mole size of pea above right hip; scar from boil on right side of neck; short scar on left side of upper lip."

In the months that followed, caring friends and acquaintances rallied. They sought her release through a pardon from President Grover Cleveland, "because the confinement she has suffered so far will be punishment of the crime and that is all that should be desired." One of her most prominent advocates was Cheyenne socialite Mrs. W.J. Cranwell. During one of Mrs. Cranwell's trips to Laramie to enlist help for her friend, she visited the felon at her cell in the state penitentiary, where Stella served as the only female prisoner during her confinement there. She "appears to be receiving most considerate treatment from the new warden [W.R. Adams]," Mrs. Cranwell later reported. "She was not compelled to cut her hair and is dressed in a calico gown of ordinary cut. She . . . does sewing for the prison as an occupation."

About a week later, a representative of the *Cheyenne Leader* visited the prison, where he found Stella:

> . . . in her cozy quarters in the southward quarter where a nice view of the mountains is offered. She is sitting at a little table, on which was a vase of pretty flowers, presented by Judge Herman Glafcke's wife, reading a book. At times she busies herself with fancy needle work and has sketched her quarters. Mrs. Gatlin was quite chipper and did not seem in the least downhearted. Of course, she was neat as a pin, as was her little home.

Having collected the signatures of some of the most influential persons in Cheyenne and Laramie on a petition calling for Stella's release, Mrs. Cranwell submitted it to Senator Joseph M. Carey. The senator, in turn, forwarded the document to the U.S. District Attorney Benjamin F. Fowler, who offered to send it along with his report to President Cleveland.

In the meantime, however, due to Stella's good conduct, she accrued seventy-five days' "good time" and gained her release from prison on December 9, 1894, by reason of expiration of sentence. She immediately left the penitentiary and returned to her home to Myersville, where she and John spent their remaining years trying to resurrect their shattered lives.

Following Stella's departure, prison officials renovated the women's ward and installed three individual cells, one of which usually served as a toilet.

SOURCES CITED

The primary source documents used in developing this story may be found in the Federal Criminal Court Case Files #104, #105, and #106, *U.S.A. v. John C. Gatlin and Stella F. Gatlin*, District of Wyoming, Eighth Judicial Circuit Court of the U.S. These records are on file at the U.S. National Archives, Rocky Mountain Branch, Denver, Colorado. Particularly helpful, too, in describing Stella's personal appearance are Wyoming State Penitentiary Inmate #150 admittance and release records on file at the Wyoming State Archives in Cheyenne. Additional information about the Gatlins' activities prior to their arrival in Wyoming may be found in a July 18, 1979, letter from Richard Johnson, Carson City, Nevada, to the Pioneer Museum in Lander, Wyoming.

Newspaper accounts, such as those contained in Cheyenne's *Daily Leader* and *Daily Sun* newspapers—from May 11, 1893 through April 13, 1894—also proved invaluable in fleshing out the intricacies of this unusual case. *Laramie Daily Boomerang* coverage of the case from April 7 through May 11, 1893, too, added perspective.

Still other sources that gave insight to the times and conditions covered by this story include Daniel Y. Meschter's *The Post Offices of Wyoming: 25 July 1868 to 31 December 1975*, compiled from "Record of Appointments of Postmasters," National Archives and Records Services Group 28, 1868 to 1931, Wyoming State Archives, Cheyenne, Wyoming.

Three Times a Loser

 Mrs. Caroline Winfield did not seem unusually disproportionate or ungainly. Still, she attracted—rather, commanded—attention. Her full bust, stooped shoulders, and five-foot, seven-inch frame, which held her 145 pounds, caught more than a few eyes. The blackness of her hair, her complexion, and, some said, her heart, caused many in predominantly "white" Wyoming to stare. But most agreed, her large, sad brown eyes, that seemed to have seen more than their fair share of troubles, drew the most attention.

Regarding her earliest life, she claimed Columbus, Ohio, as her birthplace. As a child, she probably went with her mother to Keokuk, Iowa, before moving west to Rock Springs, Wyoming. And somewhere along the route, she married—at least once—and had two children. Little else is known except that she worked as a cook to help support her family.

So on January 25, 1896, for real or imagined grievances, the twenty-seven-year-old Caroline set fire to a towel hanging on the inside wall of Jacob Berti's washhouse. When Deputy Sheriff A.E. Young learned of the crime, he rushed to the scene, where he arrested her and locked her in the local jail.

At a special two P.M. hearing about two weeks later, before the Sweetwater County Justice of the Peace W.H. Mellow, Carolina Berti swore without elaboration that Mrs. Winfield "unlawfully, maliciously, wilfully, and feloniously did attempt to burn" her husband's outbuilding.

The following morning, when court convened, Mrs. Berti and Leopold Bertagnolli repeated their stories to County and Prosecuting Attorney Elmer E. Enterline. Defended by court-appointed attorney H.R. Denton, Caroline Winfield testified on her own behalf. Based upon the prosecution's strong case, Justice Mellow found probable cause to believe Mrs. Winfield was guilty as charged. When she failed to raise bail of $250, however, authorities sent her to the county jail in Green River until the April term of the Third Judicial District Court.

Justice followed swiftly. After a brief trial in which witnesses Berti, Bertagnolli, and a man named Richard Roe testified for the State, jury foreman John Hunton declared, "We the Jury . . . so find the defendant guilty of arson as charged in the information [indictment]." Three days passed, however, before Caroline learned from Judge Jesse Knight that she must spend the next year and a half in the

Caroline Winfield-Hayes (Inmate # 259 and # 365) has the dubious distinction of being the only woman to serve more than one term in Wyoming's "Gray Bar Hotel." First she torched a Rock Springs washhouse and then she robbed a neighbor's home. Only a judge's loose leash and her fast feet saved her from a third trip to the "Big House" for stealing two blankets from a store. (Wyoming Division of Cultural Resources)

state penitentiary where, following the departure of Stella Gatlin, the authorities had remodeled the women's ward, creating three cells. There Caroline Winfield spent her hours alone in her snug, five-by-seven-by-seven-foot brick enclosure with arched ceiling and grate-iron door. Like Stella, her furnishings included a rough bed with a straw-filled mattress and a nightstand that held a chamber pot and some personal possessions. An adjacent, empty cell served as her bathroom.

In the days that followed, she also gained some feminine company. Authorities locked the notorious Minnie Snyder (Prisoner #271) into the adjoining cell on July 9, 1896, following the conviction of her and her husband Pete for killing a rancher near Marquette, Wyoming.

Thirteen months later, on August 27, 1897, with seventy-five days' "good time" to her credit, Warden Norman D. McDonald released Caroline from prison. After moving to Cheyenne, thanks to her matronly good looks and culinary skills, she soon attracted a young black suitor. On October 2, 1897, she and twenty-nine-year-old James Hayes got a marriage license and minister Sidney C. Davis married the couple in a Baptist ceremony that same day. William and Mance Kingcade of Cheyenne witnessed the nuptials.

STRIKE TWO

Their matrimonial bliss, however, lasted but briefly. Only a month and a half later, Sheriff J.P. Shaver ordered their arrest as suspects in the burglary of a neighbor, Anna Smith. Appearing on December 4 before the Laramie County Justice of the Peace W.F. Lee, the couple stood accused of entering Smith's home the previous November 13 "with the intent to steal, take and carry away the goods and chattels" there. Although Laramie County and Prosecuting Attorney Robert W. Breckons recommended James be released for lack of evidence, Caroline failed to post bail, so she was sent to the county jail. There she bided her time until the District Court of the Second Judicial District met in Cheyenne on February 17, 1898.

Caroline decided to waste neither her time nor that of the court. After she pleaded guilty to burglary as charged, Judge Charles W. Bramel instructed that she " . . . be imprisoned and confined in the Penitentiary . . . and kept at hard labor for the period of two (2) years from this date, and that during her . . . imprisonment she be clothed, subsisted and treated in all respects in accordance with the rules governing that institution, and that . . . she be safely kept untilt the term of her confinement shall be expired, or until she shall have been otherwise discharged according to law."

And so, Caroline Winfield-Hayes returned to the familiar, bare, cold cells of the state penitentiary's women's ward, where she found brief celebrity as the only woman to serve more than one sentence in that institution. But again, thanks to her good behavior, Caroline gained more "good time"—one hundred days this time—so instead of serving the full two years, she regained freedom on November 17, 1899.

"When she was discharged," reported a local newspaper, "she received the customary $5.00 from prison authorities for the immediate necessities of life and household goods . . . to enable her to live a respectable life, if she could."

A Third Time & She Was Gone

Choosing to remain in Laramie, Caroline found that life for a single woman proved hard, at best, even in a town where more than a few former criminals found refuge after doing prison time.

Struggling to survive the harsh Wyoming winter, her base instincts revived eleven days later. As a local reporter told his story:

> Caroline . . . has a sad penchant for the cup which inebriates and that is probably the cause of her present dilemma. She called at [J.H.] Davis' Second-hand store about five o'clock last evening, and observed Police Justice [J.H.] Hayford examining a pair of fifty-cent blankets. When the judge laid them down and passed on, Carrie and the blankets disappeared simultaneously. As it was between the judge and Miss Hayes, there seemed to be no doubt of which to give her the benefit, and the officers went after the woman. They found her in bed, in her room in the old Wanless building, snugly wrapped in the missing blankets. Her jag [drinking spree] would have kept her warm without any extraneous assistance, but she didn't think so.

Hayford, the Albany County Justice of the Peace, wasted no time in charging her on December 3 with petit larceny to which she acknowledged her guilt. By now as familiar with the amenities of a cell as with those offered by any rented room, Caroline remained quietly behind bars. At nine A.M. on December 5, however, she returned to court, where the judge found her guilty and sentenced her to six months in the Albany County jail.

Apparently disheartened by the latest turn of events, she pleaded for release while claiming she fully intended to return to visit her children who remained in Cheyenne. In sympathy with her circumstances, and apparently anxious to get another criminal off the Albany County rolls, Justice Hayford suspended the sentencing for twenty-four hours. She returned his favor by immediately fleeing the jurisdiction of his court.

Racing back to Cheyenne, she met with an interesting, if not spectacular, homecoming. According to the *Sun-Leader* newspaper, she "arrived from the west this morning, in an intoxicated condition. She tore her valise open and threw the contents over the floor of the ladies' waiting room, scaring the others therein almost to death."

Continuing, the reporter preached:

> The conscientious Laramie officials who talk so vigorously against the practice of shipping paupers from one town to another, better study the science of consistency. In the case above mentioned, the wench should be shipped back to the Gem City.

Counter-punching editorially, the *Laramie Boomerang* retorted:

> It will scarcely be contended that Laramie must submit to become the permanent abiding place of all the criminals who are sent to the penitentiary from the thirteen counties of the state, or even all who come from Cheyenne. All the home this Hayes woman has

on earth is in Cheyenne, and judging from developments there [gambling problems], she will at least be no discredit to it. Her husband is now living in Cheyenne; she was sent from there to the penitentiary for the crime of burglary and larceny, having previously been sent up from Green River on conviction of burning a house. It is said that Carrie is a skillful cook and in that capacity has served for several [prominent families], so she cannot properly be classed as a pauper. Cheyenne has simply come into her own. Carrie will undoubtedly feel at home over there. The atmosphere there is more congenial to her nature. The effects of the altitude here would make it inadvisable for her to return, even upon the advise of the authorities. The objections of the *Sun-Leader* are overruled.

Thanks to good Justice Hayford's loose leash and Caroline's fast feet, she took the hint by steering clear of Laramie. In fact, she seemingly disappeared, like a plume of smoke in Wyoming's wind.

Sources Cited

Sweetwater County Criminal Case File #261 and the Laramie County District Court Criminal Case File #3-512 perhaps provide the most reliable primary sources that detail Caroline Winfield-Hayes's sad story. Such documentation includes the respective Informations (Indictments), Criminal Complaints, Orders, Registers of Prisoners, and Verdicts. Additional primary sources include the Justice of the Peace Criminal Dockets for Laramie County (March 11, 1893, July 5, 1898, Vol. 3) and Albany County (1893-1903, Vol. 3); Laramie County Marriage Records (Vol. 2-5, December 2, 1874, May 14, 1896); and Sweetwater County Descriptions Lists, May 11, 1896.

And of course, the Wyoming State Penitentiary Description of Prisoner and Report of Convict Discharge records for prisoners #259 and #365 are significant, too, for information about Carolyn's physical description as well as limited background regarding her family.

Important secondary sources that provided numerous additional details about Caroline's life of crime are covered by such newspaper accounts as those in the Rock Springs *Miner* (May 14, 1896); Cheyenne's *Tribune* (May 12, 1896) and *Daily Sun-Leader* (December 8, 1898); and the Laramie *Boomerang* (November 29 and December 8, 1899).

A Shot in the Dark

THE THOUGHT MUST have crossed her mind as she sat staring into the cold glass lens: "Thank God, Pete is here to help me through this!" His warmth remained on the rough wooden stool reminding her that he had sat on this same seat moments earlier.

But now, the twenty-nine-year-old woman found herself walled away in a hostile place with a stranger, who captured her image, if not her spirit, in his brass-trimmed box. Beneath wild, wiry auburn curls, her intelligent blue eyes and tight, thin lips defied his camera. At her lean throat, an angled silver "MINNIE" pin accentuated her dress. It is the kind of portrait you might find in a trunk in your attic. The difference that can be seen on the full uncropped photo, however, are the numerals on a small sign above her right shoulder. They mark her forever as "Prisoner #271" at the State Penitentiary in Laramie.

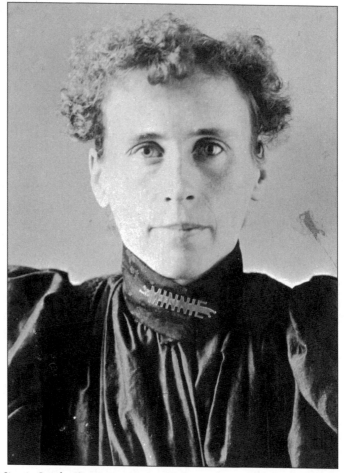

Minnie Snyder (Inmate #271) and Pete (Inmate #270), her husband, were the only married couple to be jailed concurrently in the Wyoming State Penitentiary at Laramie, Wyoming. They were housed in separate cells. They earned the "vacation" during a shootout that took the life of one of their neighboring ranchers. (Wyoming Division of Cultural Resources)

Minnie had seen better times. Much better. Born in New York about 1869, she moved as a youngster with her parents, Savina and Lewis Morgan Hulett, into the eastern part of the Dakota Territory. Then in the fall of 1881, the family—which now included another daughter, Mattie, plus sons Thomas and Morgan—moved again, this time to the northeastern part of the Wyoming Territory. Having made the winter trip with the aid of an old team of oxen, both of which sacrificed their tails to soup to keep Mr. Hulett and his party from starving to death, the family settled at the mouth of Blacktail Creek, where it empties into the Belle Fourche River. There four more siblings—Belle, Myrtle, Dona, and John—joined Minnie and her parents.

Seven years after the Huletts arrived in what is now Crook County, Mr. Hulett became the first postmaster of the small town that still bears his name. Although the life of a pioneer family rarely proved easy, Minnie seemed to enjoy a relatively happy childhood. As John D. Hale, a breeder of sheep and horses near Devils Tower, recalled, Minnie "was in my employ about one year. She was a splendid girl, very quiet and honest and I have known her for several years and never knew of a problem in her."

Later she moved to Lead City, South Dakota, where she met Pete Snyder, a rancher four years older than herself, the Kansas-born son of German parents. He was barely an inch taller than his wife, but Pete's well-muscled body contrasted greatly with her lithe frame. His large nose and teeth also seemed at odds with his wife's chiseled features. Still, they made a rather handsome couple when Justice Hall wed them on December 23, 1889, at the home of William Bogy in nearby Deadwood.

After nearly six years of marriage, Minnie announced her pregnancy with the new year as, with hopes high, they followed the sun west across Wyoming's open sky in search of their future.

Late one afternoon in 1895, they arrived in the South-fork Valley of northwestern Wyoming. Belknap Ranch hands recalled Pete and Minnie stopped their wagon, with all their worldly belongings, at a nearby river crossing. They had a sick infant. According to a witness, "Pete approached the Belknap cowboys and asked for any medication that might . . . break the baby's fever." The aid, however, proved not enough. The next morning, Pete appeared with the dead infant in his arms at the ranch house door and asked for wood to build a casket. The cook and ranch hands helped dig the baby's grave. Following the brief, simple funeral, the Snyders thanked the men and stoically returned to their wagon before driving on to their claim about thirty-eight miles southwest of Cody City.

Their baby's death signaled a sad prelude to what lay ahead. Roughly a year later, the young couple's once bright life together turned terribly bleak about 8:30 P.M. on April 2, 1896.

PEPPERED BY PELLETS

Clay McBroom, Graham Morton, and Sam Aldrich enjoyed a friendly game of whist in Aldrich's log cabin while Carl Sorenson looked on. Suddenly, a shotgun blast through the window knocked Sam to the floor. One large lead pellet

Peter Snyder (Inmate #270). (Wyoming Division of Cultural Resources)

sliced across the back of his head, seriously, but not fatally, wounding him.

By the time the men gathered their wits, treated the victim, and went cautiously outside, the would-be assassin had disappeared into the dark. With the daylight, however, their friend W.E. Pierce arrived and led them on a search that turned up the print of a woman's shoe in the moist, soft soil near the cabin. "Those tracks," they later explained, "were followed to the outer fence, where it was seen a horse had been tied. This horse, from a peculiarity in the foot, was seen to be one that Mrs. Snyder was in the habit of riding. The trail of the horse was followed and it led to the Snyder ranch" about eight miles to the northeast. Pierce claimed that "I followed the horse tracks . . . up to Mr. Snyder's barn and from there on in to the corner of there shed."

Although the men believed that, while Pete had journeyed for supplies, Minnie ambushed them and fired the shot, they did not known how to handle the situation. So while awaiting Pete's return, they sent word about the attempted murder to authorities in nearby Marquette. They then lay low while keeping the Snyders' residence under surveillance until the law could respond.

IN FEAR OF THEIR LIVES

When Pete came home and learned his and Minnie's lives might be in jeopardy, the couple decided on April 6 to drive their spring wagon the twelve miles northeast to Marquette, where they planned to seek protective custody. En route, they stopped at the ranch of John Rooks. In Rooks's absence, they "left his hired hand, Harry Jordon, the address of friends who were to be communicated with if they were killed on the way." Their misplaced trust in Jordon proved doubly ironic considering the danger they faced, because his sixty-seven-year-old friend Rooks had broken Pete's jaw in a previous altercation.

The next several hours became so steeped in confusion and controversy that the entire truth may never be known. The only testimony to survive is that of the Synders' nemeses, whose assertions are questionable, if not outright suspect.

What seems clear is that, after the Snyders left Rooks's ranch, Jordon raced to Aldrich's place, where he told Sam and his pals—Morton, Pierce, and Guss Thompson—of the Snyders' plans. Grabbing their Winchesters, Aldrich and Jordan pursued the Snyders and positioned themselves about a mile and a half ahead of the Snyders' horse-drawn wagon. The five men hoping for the quick arrival of Constable Sam Scott with arrest warrants, watched from a blind as the couple made their way toward Marquette.

Strangely and suspiciously, Rooks and William Nichols, also armed with rifles, slipped behind the Snyders' wagon, sandwiching the young couple between them and Aldrich's men. "We followed to see they did not leave the country," Bill Nichols testified later. The testimony throughout the trial was transcribed in an erratic and ungrammatical form. However, the record states Nichols said:

> Mr. Rook and I were going to Marquette We did not intend stopping them until they got to Marquette We was pretty close to Mr. Snyder when I said to Mr. Rook, 'Let's hurry up and pass Mr. Snyder' and when we got to the corner of Mr. Dyer field Mr. Snyder stoped the wagon got off on the farther side with his gun Mr. rooks he was about 20 yard ahead of me and when I seen him get of I was on the prairie I got off when I got my gun I dropped on the ground I did not have it loaded. Before I got it loaded Mr. Snyder shot at me then I fired two shots The team starded up and got to Belnap creek I see a horse I did not see Mr. Snyder any more but I could see Mrs. Snyder with her six shooter shooting toward the creek I

would not see who she was shooting at. The warrent had been sent for   our intention was to stop the parties at Marquette to await the warrent.

At the first shot, the five men, about a half mile ahead of the Snyders, immediately stopped near Belknap Creek. Moments later, a second report spun their mounts as they returned to meet the Snyders, who had halted about a half a mile east and below the creek. Suddenly an adversary's shot broke the leg of one of the couple's team, although the wounded horse managed to regain its feet. As the Snyders continued up the trail with bullets riddling their wagon, Minnie slipped from her seat while pretending to faint. Lying on their wagon bed, she busily reloaded their guns until their lame animal could go no further. Suddenly, a slug split the neck-yoke on their second horse and killed it. As Aldrich recalled:

> We rode back as fast as we could and . . . up on the side of the hill and I saw Mr. Rooks standing by a tree motioning us to come down. I rode down and tied my horse and walked up to Mr. Rooks. I asked him who started this and he said Snyder, who has shot old Bill. I got behind a tree.

During this time, Pierce and Jordon also linked up with the badly confused Rooks, who said he thought he had shot Pete Snyder.

In the meantime, after ordering Jordon to "stay with this tree," Rooks raced across the road. Said Jordon, in the poorly recorded testimony: "I tried to keep him from going, but he was bound to go. Sam Aldrich rode up close by. I said you must get down or they will kill you for I saw Mrs. Snyder telling Snyder and motioning toward Aldrich as he rode up   Sam took the tree where I was and I took another one near the creek "

ROOKS'S DEATH

As Rooks left the shelter of the cottonwood tree to trail Aldrich, Jordon said he saw a puff of smoke rise from the creek bed. Rooks fell forward on his face just before Pete, having left Minnie in the wagon, ran up along the creek. The lead ball entered Rooks's head in front of the right ear and passed out the center of the back of his head. During the following inquest proceedings, Jordon elaborated:

> I heard the report of the gun and saw the smoke and saw [Pete] Snyder directly after ward where the smoke was   I only saw Snyder fire one shot   I was about 35 yards from them then I called to Mrs. Snyder several times for them to give up there arms and they should not be hurt   she saw Snyder and he said he would give up his guns if I would agree to stay by him   then I walked out on the ice of the creek and Mrs   Snyder shot at me and I shot back at her and I went to the same tree again shortly after ward he gave up his arms.

The Snyders' antagonists rode to the nearby BN Ranch, where they got a workhorse to pull Pete and Minnie's rig to George Marquette's ranch about ten miles below on Marquette Creek. There they held the Snyders under guard while one of the captors went on to the nearest phone, about sixty miles away, at the Sirrine Ranch on Clark's Ford.

There he called the sheriff in the Black Hills, who, upon his arrival, took custody of the prisoners. On April 19, the lawman turned the Snyders over to Constable Benedict, who escorted them on to Lander, where he lodged them in jail to await their preliminary hearing.

Later, Morton and Pierce related that Pete told them he could have shot Rooks before he did, but "hated to kill the old man . . . . He had his gun on Mr. Rooks from the time he [Rooks] left the tree—the sight was pinned on his victim's head as it moved"—but Pete claimed he "did not raise the hammer until he [Rooks] was ready to shoot."

Following their capture, the weight of Rooks's corpse, plus the testimony of Aldrich and his companions, tipped the scales against the Snyders. An indictment prepared by Fremont County and Prosecuting Attorney James S. Vidal and served to Pete and Minnie at six P.M. that same day charged that they did "purposely and with premeditated malice kill and murder one John Rooks."

THE WHEELS OF JUSTICE

The prosecution filed separate criminal charges against Minnie for her alleged murderous assault on Aldrich. Due to insufficient evidence, plus confusing reassignments of justices of the peace in the Marquette Precinct, however, authorities subsequently dropped that case. Minnie still faced charges, however, as an accomplice in Rooks's death. Unable to post the required three hundred dollars bail, she returned to Sheriff Orsen Grimmett's custody, where she and Pete remained until the District Court convened at ten A.M. on June 3.

While in jail, Pete found that one of his fellow inmates carved wooden keys that might be used to open the jail doors. Fearing he and Minnie might be implicated in the scheme, Pete warned Attorney E.H. Fourt about the escape plans. Fourt, in turn, told the sheriff who searched the cells and, on May 28, found one finished key as well as "some implements used in making this . . . and also other keys in various stages of construction."

District Court Convenes in Lander

Although District Court authorities delayed their hearing because of an unusually heavy caseload, they finally brought Pete and Minnie to trial in Lander, Wyoming, on Thursday, June 11. Judge Jesse Knight sat in judgment. Thanks to attorney Fourt's intense questioning and cross-examination, the prosecution dropped its original charge of murder in the first degree and asked only for the Snyders' convictions of murder in the second degree. He settled for even less.

The presence of a woman defendant created special interest in the case and attracted sympathetic females to fill the courtroom. Three days after being seated, on Sunday, June 14, the jury reached its verdict, finding both Pete and Minnie "guilty of manslaughter."

Judge Knight first directed Pete to stand and hear his sentence. Because the justice believed Pete had fired the fatal shot, Judge Knight sentenced him to ten years in the Wyoming State Penitentiary in Laramie. He also fined Pete $1,125.10 in court costs.

The judge next ordered Minnie to rise and face the court:

The jury by their verdict have judged you guilty, but they stated that you were to be humanely treated. A woman, that is, a good woman, is respected in every community, but a woman when she uses her tongue can stir up more mischief and do more damage in a community, than any one. Of course it is well for a woman to stand by a man in times of trouble and comfort him in his distress, but for a woman to be brave enough to stand by the side of a man and taking her gun and say "I am with you," is going too far. It is one of the saddest of things to sentence a woman to the penitentiary, but my duty is so clear that I cannot escape it. I believe, in my own mind, that the country up there is as safe for a good woman to live in as anywhere. It seems strange that you and your husband have so few friends in the place you come from. The court judges that you be taken by the Sheriff of this county to the penitentiary, at or near Laramie, county of Albany, Wyoming, and that you be there confined and imprisoned for the term of six years.

IMPRISONMENT IN THE STATE PENITENTIARY

Three weeks later (July 9) Sheriff Grimmett escorted the Snyders to the State Penitentiary in Laramie, where Pete became "Prisoner #270" and Minnie joined him as "Prisoner #271."

Despite the Snyders' convictions, Attorney Fourt continued his battle for his clients' releases. When routine legal appeal procedures failed, he launched a petition and letter-writing campaign that generated literally hundreds of requests for Governor William A. Richards to pardon the Snyders. Adversaries—and there were many—soon learned of the campaign and fired their own missives to the governor.

The war of words escalated in April 1897 as a formal legal notice, published in area newspapers, announced to one and all that, at two P.M., "of said day, an application will be made to His Excellency, W.A. Richards, Governor of the state of Wyoming, at Cheyenne, Wyoming, on behalf and for the full pardon of Peter Snyder and Mrs. Minnie C. Snyder."

Upon providing the appropriate petitions and legal documents to Governor Richards, Attorney Fourt again tried to plead his clients' case:

> These people [the Snyders] if released will go directly to her folks in Crook County and to Deadwood, where he has always been able to get work.
>
> I very earnestly hope that you will find yourself able to release these people I am thoroughly certain that they are innocent.

Having summarized the evidence of the case and pointed out the prosecution's many inconsistencies, he concluded:

> Now as to the testimony of the defendants. They were absolutely uncontradicted by the little circumstances and details of the case. They were each cross-examined for a half day, and most rigidly and unmercifully. I did not try to protect them by objecting, and their testimony was absolutely unshaken. They were not caught in any particular, and though a hundred or several hundred things were brought out and then followed

with rigid cross examination, and which I had never heard of before the trial and could not have fortified them against it. They were entirely consistent. Judge Knight says he never saw as good witnesses.

Time dragged on. Despite Fourt's continued efforts, it became increasingly evident that Governor Richards, who approached the end of his term in office, did not relish possibly tarnishing that tenure by making a potentially controversial decision that favored two convicted felons. Fourt, nevertheless, sent four additional petitions signed by nearly three hundred persons from the communities of Alva, Eathen, Hulett, Sunday, and Carlile of Crook County calling specifically for Minnie's pardon. The petitioners, as friends of her family, testified,

> ... her Father and Mother are as kind in heart and as honest in purpose as are any persons in this [Crook] County. That they are among the first settlers of this County and there is not one solitary thing against their good names and that their said daughter Mrs. Minnie C. Snyder has always borne a good name in this County as much as any other person among us, and knowing her, and her parents as well as we do we cannot believe that she has ever committed any crime and especially one of such magnitude as being a party to murder. She has always been delicate and kind in disposition and affectionate to her aged parents.

No sooner had DeForest Richards succeeded W. A. Richards (no relation) in January 1899 as Governor of Wyoming than the barrage of petitions on Minnie's behalf resumed. This time her mother, Mrs. L.M. (Savina) Hulett, joined the fray to plead her daughter's case.

> If it is not asking to much will you please go to Laramie and see my daughter Minnie Snyder if you would go and talk with her I know you would be convinced that she could not be gilty of the charges against her.
>
> Her health is very poor and she can't stand confinement much longer. It is the earnest wish of a poor old mother that you will go yourself and take nobody's word but pass your judgment.

Although the Governor responded to Mrs. Hulett's request by visiting Minnie in jail, she failed to sway him enough to release her daughter.

UNTAMED MINNIE TANGLES WITH FELLOW INMATES

And so Minnie stayed in prison. Despite the "poor health" she developed there, her confinement apparently did not dull her sharp tongue. At least, it seemed that way, because on three different occasions she became involved in altercations that resulted in disciplinary actions.

The first occurred on November 11, 1900, when guards Jenkins and Hehn broke up a fight involving her and the formidable Eliza Stewart, a five-foot, seven-inch, 210-pound black woman sentenced to two years in November 1899 for felonious assault. The swearing and vulgarity that resulted landed both women in the dreaded "dark cells" for three days, with only bread and water.

Another inmate, Lillie Todd, also apparently took an intense dislike to Minnie. Lillie, imprisoned in August 1900 for grand larceny, found herself in solitary confinement on March 28, 1901, "for using vile, vulgar and profane language" to Minnie while "creating disturbance." A week later on April 6, Lillie returned to the "dark cell" and a bread and water diet, for "abusing and fighting" her redheaded jailmate.

Minnie survived those attacks, however, to be discharged from prison on August 29, 1901, "by reason of expiration of sentence. Allowed 310 days' "good time" according to law." She had served 1,511 days in prison, nearly twice as long as any other woman to be imprisoned in the Wyoming State Penitentiary.

Despite her earlier confrontations, Warden Hehn evaluated her overall conduct as "good."

POSTSCRIPT

After joining her mother in Hulett about a month and a half later, Minnie turned her attention towards seeking Pete's release by penning a note to Governor DeForest Richards.

> I will write you a few lines and I sincerely hope that you will heed them. It is in regard to my husband. I saw you and talked to you in Laramie but I was unable just after that to do what you requested me to: My sister was sick and dieing; my mother sent for me to come home; I have been here with my poor sick sister for two months and today she left us. I could not hear from my attorney Mr. Fourt but today he writes me that he had seen you. I was so in hopes I could see you again before leaving Laramie. As it is I have not been able to do one thing for my dear husband. I pray and hope you will look to it and free my boy. I did so want

him out for Christmas dinner. Please do something for him. He has been so sick in here and besides he did not deserve so many years. Please write to me and say you will help me.

I can get lots of friends here to sign a petition if you wish it. Tell me and I will circulate one, but you gave me to understand you did not wish it. Fourt says he will do all he can for me. All that will be necessary. Please do me this favor. I am so unhappy. We are all nearly heart broken and I was so in hopes my husband would be with me before this.

I hope you will tell me just what you will do. I want to send him money to come home on if you will grant this pardon. He has no money and no way of getting any. I have enough to bring him up to Deadwood and that is where I will meet him. Seriously yours. Write me at once please.

Thanks in great part to Minnie's persistence, as well as Pete's "exemplary" conduct, the Governor signed pardon papers two weeks later that authorized Pete's early release from prison on January 4, 1902. Together, they moved to Deadwood, South Dakota, where Pete worked as a miner and Minnie found employment as a housekeeper while raising a family of two boys and two girls.

Sources Cited

Many of the primary source documents used to tell this story may be found in the Fremont County District Court Criminal Case Files #228 (*State of Wyoming v. Minnie C. Snyder*) and #229 (*State of Wyoming v. Peter Snyder & Minnie Snyder*); Fremont County Coroner's Inquest re John Rooks, April 7, 1896; Board of Charities and Reform's Penitentiary Inmate Files #270 (Peter Snyder) and #271 (Minnie Snyder); Governor William A. Richards, Petitions and Pardons Files re Peter Snyder and Minnie Snyder; Governor DeForest Richards, Petitions & Pardons Files re Peter Snyder and Minnie Snyder. Ancillary materials include a letter from John D. Hale, Tilford, South Dakota, to Governor W.A. Richards, Cheyenne, Wyoming, September 12, 1897. See, too, microfilmed copies of the following newspaper accounts of the Snyders' crimes: *Sundance Gazette*, Sundance, Wyoming, December 20, 1884; the *Boomerang*, Laramie, Wyoming, June 9, 1896; the *Clipper*, Lander, Wyoming, June 12 and 19, 1896 plus April 9, 16 and 23, 1897. All these materials are on file at the Wyoming State Archives in Cheyenne, Wyoming.

Additional primary materials considered in telling this story—particularly that of the Snyders' life following their release from prison—include the 1905, 1915, 1920, and 1925 South Dakota Censuses on file at the South Dakota State Archives in Pierre, South Dakota. Also, Vernon E. Jensen's unpublished biography about Sam Aldrich (May

1958, on file at the Park County Historical Society in Cody, Wyoming) offers insight as to possible motives for the crimes.

Important secondary sources that provided additional details about Minnie's family include Mrs. Alfred H. [Cora M.] Beach's *Women of Wyoming* (Casper, WY: S.E. Boyer & Co.; 1927) and Mae Urbanek's *Wyoming Place Names* (Missoula, MT: Mountain Press Publishing Co., 1988). Regarding the crime itself, I recommend Bethene A. Larson's excellent article "Just and Probable Cause . . ." that appeared in *True West* magazine, January 1982.

Rush the Growler

"MOTHER" CURLEY knew how to turn a buck as quick as one her girls could turn a trick. More often than not, the latter made the former possible.

Referring to herself as a "boarding housekeeper," she opened a popular sporting house in 1892 at 510 W. Eighteenth Street, next to the old Cheyenne Steam Laundry in the capital city's wild west side. She also owned a cottage on Twentieth Street plus some rental properties scattered around town.

Yup, Annie did well after moving to America from her native England in God knows what year. Her entrepreneurial spirit brought her to Wyoming, where she enjoyed personal and professional opportunities not afforded her previously. Then on March 11, 1893, she married Ed Johnson in a simple civil ceremony, officiated by Justice of the Peace W.F. Lee, at her home in Cheyenne. Although we know little of Ed, we can speculate that if he found Annie appealing, big women undoubtedly held a special attraction for him. And Annie was BIG! At five feet, nine inches and 217 pounds, she probably never needed to hire a bouncer.

Although both claimed to be twenty-five years old at the time of their marriage, Annie had passed that milestone a good twelve years earlier. If the smitten Ed simply had taken time to look beyond Annie's gray eyes, he might have asked himself why more than a few strands of wispy hair of that same color draped her high forehead and framed her wide face. A skeptic might suggest that her relative prosperity offered the best cosmetic, making her small, thin lips, wedged by large ears and jowls, seem passable, if not attractive. Despite the apparent difference in their ages and her bulky appearance, they seemed happy enough . . . happy, that is, before their brief sweet life together turned sour.

The first hint of trouble came about six months into their marriage when Nannie McGonigle (or McGonagle) swore that the Johnsons and I.W. Peck burglarized the home that Nannie rented from Annie. According to the indictment issued on September 12, Laramie County and Prosecuting Attorney Van Orsdel charged the trio with stealing an eight-dollar gold ring, plus five dollars in cash from Harry Harrison, who shared Nannie's quarters. The defendants countered that while they did enter her place, they only moved her belongings out into the street after Nannie failed to pay her rent. They knew nothing, they said, about the missing items.

The prosecutor subsequently dropped the case, however, when Harrison, the key witness, left the state and attorney Van Orsdel declared "it is doubtful . . . a conviction could be sustained."

ANNIE FACES FEDERAL CHARGES

Two months later, however, Annie again found herself in hot water. This time, the federal court called her on the carpet for two counts. Benjamin F. Fowler, the U.S. District Attorney, first charged her with "selling and offering for sale beer and malt liquors, in less than five gallons at the same time, without first having paid the special tax." According to the second count, Fowler claimed she sold those beverages "without first having placed and kept conspicuously in her establishment and place of business the stamps denoting payment of the special tax."

Immediately following her arrest the next day, her friend John England promptly posted her two-hundred-dollar bail. But when Judge John A. Riner convened the next term of the Eighth Judicial District Court in Cheyenne, Annie failed to appear. Not then, at least. On January 19, 1894, Annie's physician George P. Johnston proclaimed her "pregnant (being about four months advanced) and her general temperament as one of extreme nervousness. Any slight excitement is liable to produce nervous chills and hysteria which might be followed by serious if not fatal results." Her condition, according to Doctor Johnston, made "it extremely hazardous for her to undergo the mental strain and excitement consequent upon a trial in Court." Two days later, Doctor Johnston

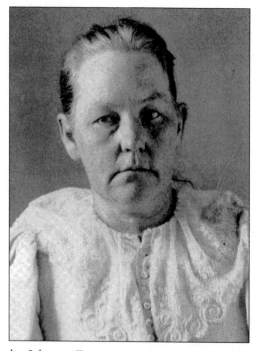

Annie Curley Johnson (Inmate #280), some say, could turn a buck as quick as one of her girls could turn a trick and, more often than not, the latter made the former possible. The large English lady lost her freedom in November 1893 for selling liquor without first paying the U.S. government's required tax. (Wyoming Division of Cultural Resources)

filed an addendum to his affidavit, stating that her condition remained "substantially the same."

Based on that diagnosis, Annie's attorneys J.C. Baird and Edmund J. Churchill succeeded in filing a Motion for Continuance, but Annie miscarried soon thereafter and needed time to recover.

When she finally came to trial on May 14, the government dropped its case against her for illegally selling liquor, and she changed her plea to guilty on the second count, a charge resulting in a fine of seventy dollars for not posting the federal tax stamp as required.

COMMISSIONER'S COURT

But her troubles continued. Once the government's spotlight touched her, its search for flaws found a character as blemished as Annie's rough complexion.

Six months after that last flap, the law served Mother Curley with still another indictment. This time Leopold Kabis, Deputy U.S. Internal Revenue Collector for the Wyoming Division of the District of Colorado, filed the complaint. He claimed Annie again sold retail liquor without having paid federal tax.

The following day (December 13, 1895), U.S. Marshal John A. McDermott and his deputy J.A. Breckons arrested Annie and brought her, bundled against Wyoming's cold winter winds, before her former lawyer, Churchill, now Commissioner of the U.S. Circuit Court for the District of Wyoming. Consider the ironies. Annie found herself face to face with a member of the same legal team that defended her against previous federal charges. But this time, following her arraignment, she pleaded "not guilty" on the advice of her new attorney—her past nemesis and former U.S. District Attorney Benjamin F. Fowler. Neither attorney apparently considered "conflict of interest" a detriment to justice. Nevertheless, Commissioner Churchill found it his task, as he convened his court that day, to determine whether sufficient evidence existed to warrant trying Annie on those charges before the U.S. Federal District Court.

Prosecuting Attorney Gibson Clark first called the government's witnesses to the stand. A. John Wilson had arrived in the Cheyenne area six weeks earlier, after leaving his home on Powder River in Johnson County to break horses for rancher R.S. Van Tassell. His cowpuncher friends Charles Workentine and Frank Stewart seemed well acquainted with the city and its hot spots. Charley, a Cheyenne resident for more than eight years, said he visited Annie's place off and on for five years. He added that he knew she "had kept the place for the past three or four." Frank boarded at the Sherman House for about six months.

According to John, he went about "half past nine or eight" on Tuesday, December 10, with Charley, Frank, and Mollie, a good time girl, to Annie's place, where from seven to thirteen other people stopped by to drink and party. Charley added, they "had a little music, danced a little" before calling for some drinks. "We first had beer," he said. Then Mollie, who claimed that she "can't drink beer," pulled Addie Wilson, Annie's black cook, aside and asked for some whiskey "on the quiet." Addie replied that first she had to check with Mrs. Johnson.

After stepping briefly into a back room, Addie returned and ushered the group into a private front room off the parlor, where she sold and served them four dollars' worth of liquor.

Fannie, "a big tall girl," soon joined the group and they retired to a room that Fannie rented from Annie. She previously had been in the dining room with Annie and Ruth

Stanton. Ruth, like Fannie, Hazel Clifton, Kittie Gilbert, and Lizzie Weaver, all rented rooms in Annie's establishment. Unlike Mollie, Fannie never drank anything but beer. "There isn't any of the girls but me," she bragged, "that can play the piano as good."

After making its point that Annie illegally sold liquor, the government rested its case. Defense Attorney Fowler next called his first witnesses. After taking the stand, Annie said she arrived at the house on Eighteenth Street "along the first of the evening, for part of the evening after dark; we have supper at 6 P.M. I think it was about that time. I probably left the house about 7 P.M."

Although Annie denied either keeping beer and liquor or selling such beverages to anyone at her establishment, she acknowledged that Addie told her that she had sold drinks that night. She said, according to Addie, that Mollie "asked ... if she could have some drinks; I told her 'yes' in the girls room." When challenged about the propriety of that act, Annie said, "The girls rent the rooms from me; if they want beer in their own rooms they can have it I suppose; they pay me straight room rent and I don't know why they can't have beer in their own rooms ... They can do what they want to in their rooms."

Annie closed by telling attorney Fowler that after she left the building about ten P.M., she did not return again that night.

ADDIE'S DAY IN COURT

Fowler next called Addie Wilson to the stand. The cook said she worked for Annie for six weeks and lived at a place on Nineteenth Street. "Sometimes I stay at my house at night," she testified, "and sometimes I stay at Mrs. Curley's."

On the night in question, Addie said that when the customers asked for beer:

> We took up a collection and I went out and got the beer . . . in a big 10 pound tin bucket . . . when we went into Miss Fannie's room we rushed the growler . . . Miss Fannie got a quarter's worth of beer and says I could have the other quarter for going after it.

> This Brown girl said that beer wasn't strong enough for her; she wanted something stronger; so I said 'Miss Fannie' I have got some whiskey to take home for my husband [who had been] away hunting and I had been looking for him and was uneasy about him; so I thought I would get something to surprise him; he had hurt his foot [about six months earlier] and the doctor told me whiskey would do it good so I got the whiskey . . . Doctor [W.W.] Crook said it would be good for his foot to rub it in whiskey. He liked the whiskey all right; he is drunk now.

It is likely her testimony caused a few in the crowded court to yearn for a drink themselves. As the winter sun beamed through the tall windows and warmed the room, the closeness of it all caused some to sweat and fidget. Addie continued:

> I had a little jug and I went down [about four P.M., on the 10th] to the Idelman's [store] to get some whiskey for him to drink and some to put on his feet and some to make mince meat of and I said they could have some of that.

The clerk . . . is a low heavy set man with a black moustache and very heavy eyebrows; he wasn't so very heavy set . . . about Mr. Churchill's build only not so tall . . . a little bit of whiskers coming out like a man who hadn't shaved for a while, for two or three days say.

According to Addie, the clerk said, "You got enough for the old man?"

"Yes, I got enough; I wanted it to rub his foot with and a little for him to drink; a little of that will set a man crazy."

The clerk said, "It would burn me up."

Under continued examination by attorney Fowler, Addie acknowledged that she borrowed the money from Fannie to buy the whiskey. She claimed, however, that Annie knew nothing of the deal.

Addie, testifying further, said she had the liquor in the "library," where she occasionally slept.

There is a lot of books in it; I sleep there when I don't go home. I put it in my room in a closet that is there; a closet where Mrs. Curley keeps her clothes; I have a key to this room and she has a key to it too; so I says all right and went in to the closet; the girls came on in to my room with me and we took the jug; I couldn't pour the whiskey out of the jug and so I went out in the dining room and got a milk pitcher and poured it out into the pitcher and poured it from the pitcher into the glasses.

When I had done this Miss Fannie says to the boys I think we ought to give Addie something, something that way for her whiskey so the men throwed out some money (looking towards the defendants) . . . I don't know his name—he throwed down a dollar on the server [tray] these two men gave me to dollars and I put the two dollars in my pocket; Fannie called it luck money.

According to Addie, "I was getting tired; when she came back she told me it was getting pretty noisy in there and she called Miss Fannie out of the room and said, 'Fannie, you must not make so much noise.' She had only been at the house for about five minutes when "she told me to take care of the house; she wanted to be with Mr. Johnson all she could because he was going away . . . on the 3 A.M. train."

A RETURN TO FEDERAL DISTRICT COURT

Toward the end of the testimony, it took no seer with a crystal ball to read Annie's bleak future. Members of the Commissioner's Court concluded that sufficient evidence existed—thanks as much to the defense's witnesses as to those presented by the prosecutor—to continue Annie's case before the Federal District Court of the Eighth Judicial District when it convened its next term at the State Capitol in Cheyenne.

On May 11, Federal District Attorney Clark entered a revised indictment against Annie. It charged that Annie did "wilfully, knowingly and unlawfully exercise and carry on the business of a retail liquor-dealer by selling and offering for sale foreign and domestic distilled spirits, wines and malt liquors in less quantities than five gallons at a time, without first having paid the special tax therefore as is required by the statute of the United States in that behalf, with intent . . . to defraud the United States."

In the meantime, the prosecutor developed new evidence and subpoenaed additional witnesses to include three Company D, Eighth Infantry soldiers from nearby Fort D.A. Russell: John Gambrel, James L. Ewing, and Casper C. Hamilton. Once again, U.S. Marshal McDermott brought Annie before the court that same day to answer those men's accusations.

Given her track record and the troopers' damning testimony, it took little time or effort for the jury to reach its verdict. On July 22, its members found her "guilty as she stands charged in the indictment." When Annie offered no comment regarding the decision, Judge Riner pronounced sentence: that she pay a fine of one hundred dollars and be confined in the penitentiary at Laramie "for the period of one year and one day from this date."

Marshal McDermott escorted Annie the following day to Laramie, where, during her incarceration in prison, she shared the female department with four other women convicts: Caroline Winfield-Hayes, Minnie Snyder, Eliza "Big Jack" Stewart, and Lillian Todd. Finally, after she earned fifty days' "good time," authorities discharged her on June 2, 1897.

Where did she go? What did she do? Only history holds answers to those secrets.

SOURCES CITED

The usage "rush the growler," meaning to fetch beer in a pail, was popular between 1888 and 1903, according to the *Random House Historical Dictionary of American Slang* (Lighter, 1994). Partridge's *Concise Dictionary of Slang and Unconventional English* notes that "growler" derives from the "growling of the beer taps."

The primary source documents used in developing this story include the Justice of the Peace Docket Book, Laramie County, March 11, 1893 and July 5, 1893; Laramie County Criminal Case File #3-414, *State of Wyoming v. Annie Curley Johnson, Ed Johnson & I.W. Peck*; Transcript of Hearing, Commissioner's Court, Federal Criminal Court Case File #116, *U.S.A. v. Annie Curley Johnson*, District of Wyoming, Eighth Judicial Circuit Court of the U.S., December 12, 1895; and Wyoming Board of Charities and Reform State Penitentiary, Convict #280 files. Also, the Marriage Records, March 11, 1893, Laramie County Clerk, Vol. 3, provided details regarding Annie's marriage to Ed Johnson, while the *Cheyenne City Directory*, 1895, helped more fully identify characters and locations mentioned in this story. These documents may be found in the Wyoming State Archives.

Additional primary information, contained in Federal Criminal Court Case Files #116 and #156, *U.S.A. v. Annie Curley Johnson*, District of Wyoming, Eighth Judicial Circuit Court of the U.S., is on file in the U.S. National Archives, Rocky Mountain Branch, Denver, Colorado.

"Big Jack" Was No Lady

SOME JEST THAT LIKE Topsy, Harriet Beecher Stowe's character in *Uncle Tom's Cabin*, Eliza Stewart probably "just growed." Others facetiously say some primal force cast her up like a crude lump of coal from a vein beneath the dry, bare plain there in Carbon County. In fact, history has forgotten how she got to Hanna, Wyoming, although she may have been among the two hundred black men and women brought from Harrison County, Ohio, in January 1890, to work the coal mines near Hanna.

What is known is that the rough, flawed Eliza had skin the color of deep, bituminous coal. The native of Greensboro, Alabama, used narcotics and sometimes carried a gun beneath her smock . . . not attributes of a lady, particularly just prior to the turn of the century. Still, she had an elementary education, attended the Baptist Church when the spirit moved her, and made her way as a housekeeper. And Eliza usually did not go hungry as the 210 pounds on her five-foot, five-inch frame attested.

The good times, however few, came to an end on July 16, 1899, at a Saturday night dance in Hanna. No one called her mean or quarrelsome. Given her addiction to morphine, that drug probably made her euphoric, perhaps oblivious to events around her. But something . . . someone ignited her. Though usually slow to burn, she exploded this night like mine gas.

Details are sketchy. What is known is that "Big Jack," as many called her, walked up to a black man named David Glenn. As the music played, she pulled a revolver from beneath the folds of her ample apron and shot him in the neck. A lovers' spat? A quarrel over money? One guess is as good as another.

The following morning, J.J. Friedman, a Carbon County deputy sheriff, filed an official complaint with Edw. McAtee, the Hanna Precinct justice of the peace. He charged Eliza with attempting to murder Glenn with a "pistol . . . loaded with powder and leaden pellets." Later that day, as Deputy Friedman took Eliza into custody, others prepared the wounded Glenn for his trip to Rock Springs. There Dr. R. Harvey Reed successfully treated him that Monday afternoon in the hospital and reported, still later, to Carbon County and Prosecuting Attorney Homer Merrell that his patient "was getting along all right."

When she appeared on July 19 before Justice McAtee, although Eliza pled "not guilty," conflicting testimony from other witnesses convinced the judge to find the charges were

Eliza "Big Jack" Stewart, Inmate #459, addicted to morphine, shot a man in the throat during a Saturday night dance in Hanna, Wyoming. Although he survived, she spent the next twenty-one months cooling her heels in the Wyoming State Penitentiary for committing that crime. (Wyoming Division of Cultural Resources)

valid and to bind her over for trial. When she failed to pay the five-thousand-dollar bail, the court remanded her to the care of the keeper of the county jail, where they kept her pending her appearance before the Third District Court in Rawlins.

The next day, Deputy Friedman took Eliza to Rawlins where, following her arraignment, the judge locked her up and appointed N.R. Greenfield to serve as her defense attorney. As Eliza quietly awaited her fate, Carbon County and Prosecuting Attorney Merrell gathered evidence and prepared his case against her. In the meantime, Glenn's condition so improved that by August 2, Doctor Reed reported that he [Glenn] "will be discharged in a few days."

Finally, on October 18, Merrell submitted an indictment in which he swore that Eliza:

> . . . unlawfully, wilfully, maliciously, feloniously, purposely and with premeditated malice, having the present ability to do so, in and upon the person of one David Glenn make an assault, and did in a rude, insolent and angry manner unlawfully touch the said David Glenn, and with a certain pistol, which she . . . had and held, to at, and against . . . Glenn, did shoot off with the intent then and there to commit a felony, to wit: with intent then and there to kill and murder.

This time E.M. Horton, another Carbon County deputy, delivered the court's complaint to Eliza. Again she pled "not guilty."

SWIFT JUSTICE

Eliza, whose trial began October 28, soon learned the swiftness, as well as the sureness, of Wyoming justice. After the convincing testimony of the recovering Glenn, as well as that from James Tennant, Louise Wideman, William "Willie" King, and Dr. J.C. Hammon, the case went to the jury at noon without argument by either the prosecutor or the defense attorney. Within minutes the jurors rendered their verdict: "guilty of felonious assault with intent to commit manslaughter." Judge D.H. Craig, who sentenced Eliza, spared her the maximum sentence of fourteen years, opting instead to give her two years at "hard labor" in the Wyoming State Penitentiary.

The following day, County Sheriff Creed McDaniel escorted his prisoner to neighboring Albany County, where he delivered her to prison authorities in Laramie. With a ring of the bell that had also welcomed her seven female predecessors, Eliza entered through the great, iron-trimmed door in the west wall of the prison, where guards greeted her as "Inmate #459."

As one scans the photos of all the women who served time there, Eliza's mug shot is clearly the most memorable . . . imposing. The term "dominating" comes to mind. Her girth, accentuated by the large plaid pattern of her dress, demands attention while she stares contemptuously through narrowed, flinty eyes. Her large, full lips show no remorse. Although the small pearls that hang from her pierced ears lend a distinctive feminine touch, a man's dark fedora perches incongruously atop her head. It is skewered squarely to her neatly coiffed hair by a long hat pin. With only the open aperture of his camera separating him from the large, intimidating woman, the photographer swiftly snapped his shutter, thus ending the sitting.

Her intimidating persona probably faded under the hospital doctor's physical examination that revealed her most intimate secrets: "a mole on left side of neck, one front tooth out, has a large cut scar back of neck, a small scar on center of forehead over nose, large breasts."

With the degrading in-processing over, she entered under guard into the South Wing of the prison and proceeded to the southeast corner of the second tier. There she discovered Caroline Winfield-Hayes and Minnie Snyder. Authorities released Caroline just three days later. But Minnie, who had been serving time there since July 9, 1896, for manslaughter, remained even after Eliza ended her sentence.

The following August, still another woman, Lillie Todd (Inmate #510), joined their little group. Although each of the women had her own cell, they shared a common bathroom installed in an adjoining cubicle.

It may have been the stark, brutal conditions there, or an inevitable clash of personalities—possibly both—but Eliza and Minnie locked horns on Sunday morning, November 11, 1900. Regardless of what started the fray, their guards Jenkins and Hehn reported them for "swearing and vulgarity with much noise" to Warden T. Jeff Carr. The warden, in turn, sent them into the "dark cells" for three days, serving them only bread and water. Each woman also lost five days of her coveted, hard-earned "good time" for that offense.

Eliza apparently learned her lesson, because on July 20, 1901, Warden Carr restored her five days' "good time" "for [her] extra work and good conduct."

She also found freedom on August 4, the following month, having accumulated 100 days' good time, the most she could accrue given her sentence. And she apparently learned to avoid future trouble, because she drifted away in Wyoming's wind as unobtrusively as she arrived.

SOURCES CITED

The primary source documents used to develop this story may be found in the Carbon County Third District Court Criminal Case File #429, *Wyoming v. Eliza Stewart*; Wyoming State Penitentiary file and mug shot regarding Prisoner #459; and Wyoming Charities and Reform, State Penitentiary Disciplinary Record, May 1892-October 1906, that are on file at the Wyoming State Archives.

Important secondary sources include T.A. Larson's superb *History of Wyoming* (Lincoln, Nebraska: University of Nebraska Press, 1978); The *Journal* newspaper, Rawlins, Wyoming, July 19-28 and October 1899; the *Rawlins Republican*, Rawlins, Wyoming, July 22 and October 21, 1899. *The Visitors' Guide* to the Wyoming Territorial Park in Laramie, Wyoming, provides an informative contemporary overview of that facility.

A Callous Lillie

SHORTLY AFTER LUNCH on Monday, August 6, 1900, a neat, trim, coffee-colored lady entered the Vendome Hotel at 102 W. Eighteenth Street in Cheyenne, Wyoming. A wide black ribbon tied elegantly about the crown accentuated her fashionable, coarse-woven straw hat. And upon the bow perched a large artificial calla lily, symbolic of her name: Lillie, Lillie Todd.

Wandering through the halls as if she owned them, she answered offers of help by saying that she only sought the landlady. Dressed smartly in a crisp smocked shirtwaist, a tailored jacket of dark cloth, tiny button earrings, plus that striking hat, Lillie seemed to belong in this hotel and no one seemed the wiser. Only her unnatural calm, and the odd, pinpoint pupils of her large, sad, dark brown eyes, might have betrayed her real mission. She sought something of

Lillie Todd (Inmate #510), a wife, mother, and trained nurse, turned to a life of crime to support her craving for drugs. When that failed, she found herself in prison, where, because of her bad behavior, authorities found it repeatedly necessary to confine her to the "dreaded dark cell." (Wyoming Division of Cultural Resources)

value that could be sold or traded to feed her master: morphine. Whether by chance or design, the twenty-eight year-
old visitor found her way about 2:30 P.M. to the room of
Claude and Isabella Draper, absent from the hotel at that
time. Within seconds, Lillie entered their unlocked suite
and pinched a pair of diamond earrings, a diamond pin, and
a gold ring.

After slipping out of the building that afternoon, she
worked her way about ten blocks east to N.H. Andrus's Jewelry Store at 917 E. Sixteenth Street. There she offered to
sell part of her ill-gotten gain to the watchmaker. She said
she needed the money "to send a sick friend away." Not one
to pass up a "steal," Andrus quickly gave her $7.50 for the
obviously valuable jewelry.

Later Mrs. Draper returned to her room, but not until
9:30 P.M. did she notice her gems missing. She immediately
called the law. Armed with a detailed description by the
hotel staff of its prime suspect, the police lost no time in
checking the key exits from town. Sure enough, fifteen minutes later, they found Lillie at the south end of Capitol
Street in the Union Pacific depot. There, she awaited the
coal burning train that she hoped would return her to her
husband, William, and their little girl awaiting her at their
home in Laramie. Instead, authorities arrested Lillie and,
after relieving her of what remained of her ill-gotten loot,
they took her to the Laramie County Courthouse at the corner of Ferguson and Nineteenth Street. They booked her
before locking her away in the adjacent jail, where she
curled the 115 pounds of her small-boned frame upon a
stiff, straw mattress. Although shamed by being caught, she

knew even worse lay ahead. As a trained nurse, she undoubtedly feared most the loss of that artificial sense of well-being brought on by a needle full of morphine. And "cold turkey" withdrawal from the drug could be hell.

Fortunately for Lillie, a speedy trial helped distract her from the pain that probably left her irritable and angry. Within a few hours of her arraignment, the Laramie County Attorney and Prosecutor H. Waldo Moore issued an indictment charging her with grand larceny, and she went before Justice of the Peace John A. Martin. Faced with a crime she knew to be true, she simply chose to plead "guilty." Unable to post the one-thousand-dollar bail ordered by Justice Martin to help assure her appearance before the district court, she waived her rights and opted for immediate sentencing. The good judge obliged by giving her one year in the Wyoming State Penitentiary.

PRISON BOUND

That Wednesday [August 8] Sheriff John P. Shaver escorted his prisoner back to the depot where, this time, they boarded the westbound train for Laramie. As the deep black pits in the centers of her eyes grew large with the lack of her drug, Lillie fought the sun's harsh rays that poured through the windows of the passenger car. Arriving in Laramie that afternoon, the sheriff loaded his prisoner into the same horse-drawn wagon that he used to carry so many of her predecessors across the bridge over the Laramie River to the state penitentiary.

Upon entering the fortress's gray walls, the cool, filtered light most probably gave Lillie's hot, sore eyes relief for the first time since her arrest. Her peace ended quickly, however, because the guard immediately led her down the corridor to the prison processing room, where the five-foot, two-inch Lillie signed in as "Convict #510." Although more than one thousand prisoners had preceded her into the prison since it opened in January 1873, it is likely she soon learned that only eleven women had been there before her.

At the in-processing desk, the clerk and a prison physician discovered the most personal details about their new prisoner. Born in Michigan, Lillie claimed the Catholic faith and said she enjoyed a "fair" education as a child. Despite her addiction to narcotics, the clerk listed her "Habits of Life" as "Temperate" before turning her over to the doctor who examined her lithe body for identifying scars and marks: "Small cut scar under chin on right side. Small mole on left side of nose . . . Features regular. Good teeth." Before the attending photographer snapped her mug shot, a prison administrator told her that while doing time for her crime, she might earn as many as fifty days "good time." In other words, if she kept her nose clean and obeyed the rules, she could serve as few as 315 days of her one-year sentence. *Could*, but wouldn't.

After completing the necessary paperwork, Lillie's guard led her upstairs, where he locked her in a cell adjoining those of the infamous Eliza "Big Jack" Stewart (Convict #459) and Minnie C. Snyder (Convict #271).

NOT A NICE LADY

Regrettably, the monastic life did little to blunt Lillie's temper. In fact, of all the petticoat prisoners who served time there, authorities found reason to punish Lillie more frequently and more severely than any other. The first incident happened September 25 about seven weeks after they locked her up. Guard J.P. Hehn caught her and convict Thomas Tracy (Convict #498) writing notes to each other. He also found them guilty of having unauthorized lead pencils. For those violations, he locked Lillie in her cell and fed her nothing but bread and water from nine A.M. that day until he let her out of her cage at four P.M. two days later. Lillie also lost "five days good time." Tracy received comparable punishment.

Within five months, Lillie earned still more discipline. Guard Hillenbrand claimed she used "vile, vulgar and profane language to convict Mrs. Snyder" while "creating a disturbance." Apparently believed to be the aggressor, the new warden W.R. Adams tossed Lillie—not Minnie—into solitary confinement. She remained in solitary from eight A.M. on March 28, 1901, until a guard returned her to her cell at eleven A.M. the following morning. One evening about a week later, Lillie again attacked Minnie. This time, after guard Herrell broke them up, Warden Adams apparently decided to teach Lillie a lesson. Back she went into solitary confinement. She remained there from 7:20 P.M. on April 6 until 7:30 A.M. the next day when they returned her to her cell, but the bread and water diet continued by order of the warden until April 9 when they again served "regulation food" to her. They did not permit her to resume her normal prison schedule, however, until April 13. These last two incidents cut an additional ten days from her "good time" credit.

Had her conduct been better, Lillie might have been out of the stir as early as June 17. But given her temper and unwillingness to abide by the rules, she remained in the pen until July 2, 1901, when she finally gained her release "by reason of expiration of sentence." Presumably—and hopefully—Lillie rejoined her husband and child to rebuild her once good life. Returning to her old lover, "Mr. Morphine," would have been the cruelest fate.

Sources Cited

The primary source documents used to develop this story may be found in the Laramie County District Court Criminal Case File #4-13, *State of Wyoming v. Lillie Todd* plus Wyoming State Penitentiary files, the records and mug shot for Prisoner #510, Prisoner Disciplinary Records of the Wyoming Board of Charities and Reform (Vol. I, May 1892-October 1906, p. 216), and the Laramie County Prison Calendar 1881-1908, p. 8, that are on file at the Wyoming State Archives.

Additional sources of the time that provided important information about this case include the *Cheyenne City Directory* (Cheyenne, WY: Tribune Press, Greeley, CO), August 1902, and the *Cheyenne Daily Leader*, August 7, 1900, p. 4.

Sisters in Sin

PEARL AND GERTIE Smith claimed to be sisters, but they lied. They shared, however, a love of the fast life and a past that left an indelible mark, staining Wyoming's criminal history.

It all started innocently enough. Pearl entered this world about 1882 in Illinois, where she shared the home of her parents Mr. and Mrs. Ben Smith with two older sisters. Shortly after Pearl's birth, the Smiths moved to Denver, Colorado, where a fourth daughter—Clara—joined the family three years later.

Pearl, according to her mother, "was always the best of daughters," even turning over all the money she earned as a Hewitt Candy Company employee to help support her family. A.A. Bodine also remembered her fondly as "an honest respectable young lady" during the two years she worked for

Pearl Smith (Inmate #680) left her husband in Kansas City, Missouri, and turned to Joseph Murphy, who became her lover and companion in a life of crime that landed both of them in the Wyoming State Penitentiary. (Wyoming Division of Cultural Resources)

Joseph Murphy (Inmate #682). (Wyoming Division of Cultural Resources)

him at his Big Four Oyster House. She even found time to gain a common basic elementary education and attend Sunday services periodically at the local Baptist Church.

All in all, things seemed to be going fairly well for the poor, but respected, family. Well, that is, until Pearl turned sixteen and married Claude Bowman, a young mechanic from Kansas City. Although little else is known of her husband, the young wife apparently reveled in her new found freedom. Regrettably, the novelty of her new role soon waned. Although rid of her family's strict influence and demands, those of her husband apparently seemed just as restrictive and frustrating. Regardless of the reason, Pearl failed to be restrained. Within a year, she deserted Claude and turned her pale blue eyes toward the west.

GERTIE SMITH

It is not known when or how Pearl and Gertie Miller got together. What is known is that Gertie adopted Pearl's maiden name, and they joined ranks as sisters in sin. They even shared clothes as each stood five feet, five and a half inches tall and weighed about 120 or 130 pounds. They wore their hair in a similar style—soft, high and parted in the middle—and favored frocks with fussy collars buttoned at the throat. And their addiction to bright lights and drugs seemed to rival their attraction for men with troubled lives.

Despite such similarities, Pearl's regular features and small mouth looked tight and pinched when compared to Gertie's full, sensuous lips, long nose, and cleft chin.

Regardless, the sisters "Smith" spelled trouble from the start. Gertie first gained official attention when she and James Martin "were driven out" of Cripple Creek, Colorado, for various nefarious deeds. Authorities later chased them out of Denver. It is believed that Pearl and a thirty-four-year-old Irish rogue from Ohio named Joseph Murphy joined them in that departure.

Toward the end of April 1902, the quartet appeared at Fort Steele, an army post east of Rawlins, where they spent about three weeks.

Pearl's beau, Murphy, seemed relatively well educated, having attended "normal school." He worked occasionally as a tailor and knew how to show a girl a good time. Despite his broken nose and the 191 loosely packed pounds about his five-foot, six-inch frame, he cut a rather dashing figure with his warm, light blue eyes and graying hair. He even sported a couple of colorful tattoos, including a red and blue "Indian Maiden" on his arm. It mattered little to Pearl that Joe's wife, Bridget, and their two children—a boy and a girl—waited for him in Minneapolis, Minnesota.

And their friend, twenty-three-year-old James Martin, had Gertie in tow. The well-built James, who claimed Gertie as his "wife," appeared handsome in a lean, mean sort of way. A native of Michigan, the five-foot, nine-inch cook had chestnut-colored hair and hard blue eyes that tended to turn a dull grey under the influence of his nemeses: drugs and alcohol.

LIGHT-FINGERED MURPHY LANDS THEM IN JAIL

Despite the good times this quartet shared, their high life came to a screeching halt one afternoon in Rawlins, Wyoming. Arriving there on Friday, May 16, 1902, they checked into the Willis Rooming House. They planned to loot some homes the next day while the circus in town diverted the local folks' attention from the strangers' activities.

When the traveling menagerie failed to show, James strolled down to the Club Saloon, where he spent the day drinking and playing cards. Joe and the Smith girls, in the meantime, went shopping. Their *modus operandi* seemed to work relatively well. Entering the store of J.W. Hugus, Gertie and Pearl engaged the clerks by making small purchases while Joe stuffed three pairs of corduroy pants under his coat.

At the Golden Rule store, operated by D.A. Larson and L.M. Callahan, the thieving trio struck more gold, so to

Gertie Miller (Inmate #681), the second "Smith Sister," linked up with James Martin in a relationship that not only cost them their freedom, but led to the loss of her life during the birth of their child. (Wyoming Division of Cultural Resources)

James Martin (Inmate #683). (Wyoming Division of Cultural Resources)

speak. There, Joe filched two fur scarves, two silk dress waists, two cotton shirtwaists, and a handkerchief, the total valued at $22.81.

Their greed, however, finally tripped them up at the Rawlins Mercantile Company. As Joe tried to snitch a silk dress shirt, a dress waist, three dress shirts, and a pair of muslin drawers, one of the shirts fell from beneath his coat. According to a witness's later testimony, "Mrs. M.E. McIntosh saw the garment lying on the floor and thought it had been knocked off the counter. Later a couple of shirtwaists were picked up on the street," where Joe dropped them. That night, he shipped a valise filled with their loot via the number five train to Rock Springs for safekeeping.

In the meantime, the stores' managers alerted authorities, who arrested James when he returned to his room that evening. After hauling him off to jail, an officer stayed at the rooming house, where he nabbed Pearl and Gertie when they returned. Inside their room, he found a stolen twenty-five-dollar silk skirt hanging behind the door.

Joe, however, evaded the police until the following day. While walking the street, Walter and Norrie France recognized a fellow stroller as the same man "who was in the stores with the women." City Marshal William Healy and Deputy Sheriff E.M. Horton immediately rushed to the scene, where they found Joe hiding in a culvert at the west end of town. He refused, at first, to come out until the officers pulled their guns.

During his subsequent investigation, Sheriff Creed McDaniel learned of Joe's shipment the previous evening and went to Rock Springs to investigate. There, in the valise, he found most of Joe's loot, which he later returned to the rightful owners.

Four days later [May 22], the justice of the peace in Rawlins indicted and tried the four defendants, who pled "not guilty" only to be bound over for trial before the District Court of the Third Judicial District. Returning to the bleak Carbon County jail, they remained in their cells until June 3 when the District Court convened.

Considering the evidence, as well as their soiled reputations, court-appointed attorney N.R. Greenfield warned his clients that a long legal battle awaited them if they chose to fight. Besides, he suggested, the presiding judge, D.H. Craig, enjoyed a lenient reputation. Encouraged by Greenfield's optimism, they bowed to their lawyer's advice and changed their pleas to "guilty." Judge Craig, however, surprised them by showing no mercy. Instead, he threw the book at them and condemned them to the new Wyoming State Penitentiary there in Rawlins. Without explanations regarding the disparities in their sentences, he gave Pearl two years in the slammer; Gertie got four years; Joe received five years; and poor James, the innocent, found himself facing six years.

Later that day, Sheriff McDaniel escorted the two couples across town, through the great gate, and into the bristling barbed-wire compound at the north side of Rawlins, Wyoming. Under the watchful eyes of the armed turret guards, they crossed the bare yard to an iron-trimmed door, where their escort pulled a bell rope to announce their arrival. After a few moments, a huge metal key turned within the lock on the far side of the port, and the armed sentry who admitted them re-locked the door immediately after they entered. After being taken directly to the prison's processing room, authorities there asked the prisoners their names, ages, and backgrounds as well as information about their families, past occupations, religions, and levels of education. They also questioned the new inmates about their temperance—whether they had been promiscuous or had used drugs and alcohol. After being weighed and posed for prison identification photos, the new "residents" disrobed for a doctor, who measured them, determined their physical characteristics, and examined them for scars as well as other identifying marks.

Next, officials cropped short the men's hair and issued them special, drab garb before locking them away in A-Block, the men's wing of the prison. Authorities permitted the women prisoners, however, to keep their long hair and wear whatever garments friends and relatives provided.

In addition to the dress code, other significant differences existed between the handling of male and female convicts. For example, well-behaved men might enjoy more diversity in their labors, because they worked in the prison factory, labored in the field, and tended livestock. They also dined en masse and shared the relative luxury of exercising together.

After in-processing, a guard led the ladies through a long, dark corridor to the main lobby of the prison administration building and up two flights of stairs. Upon reaching the third floor, they entered a fifteen-foot, four-inch by eighteen-foot chamber. The north wall of the women's ward in this new state penitentiary had three individual cells with a small, common-use sink and toilet wedged into the northeast corner of the room.

Unlike the men, the women found themselves confined to their ward, where they ate, mended, washed clothes, and slept. Such isolation must have been terrible, but violation of the non-fraternization code could be worse. A petticoat prisoner caught breaking that rule might lose the "good time" she accrued. Worse, the "dark cell" concept was enforced at this new ward as well.

Although well lit by a barred window on the west and two more ports on the north, the ward's iron-plated interior and gritty stone floor seemed depressingly cold, particularly in the early spring and winter. A small steam radiator near the barred door offered little comfort. A medical bay of nearly the same size, lay east and across the stairwell. A

The Wyoming State Penitentiary in Rawlins, Wyoming, officially opened the doors of its first cellblock on December 12, 1901. Although authorities planned to phase out its predecessor pen at Laramie, unanticipated crowding and an outbreak of smallpox at the new prison delayed that action. Consequently, officials kept open the old pen in Laramie and designated it as the Wyoming State Auxiliary Penitentiary. It remained as such until June 4, 1903, when its last seventeen prisoners were transferred to Rawlins and incarcerated there. (Wyoming Division of Cultural Resources)

fifty-foot by seventy-two-foot chapel, the largest room on that floor, dominated the southern part of the building. Harsh hymns sung by whiskey baritones and droning Sunday sermons may have seemed as painful to the women as the cries they heard from the small hospital.

In fact, their proximity to male medical patients soon posed "a management problem," so within approximately three weeks following the Smith Sisters' conviction authorities transferred them by guard to the old pen in Laramie. Authorities had kept it open as the Wyoming Auxiliary State Penitentiary when unanticipated crowding and an outbreak of smallpox created a need for more space soon after the official opening of the Wyoming State Penitentiary in Rawlins on December 12, 1901.

GREENFIELD PLEADS FOR THEIR PARDONS

During the next several months, attorney Greenfield felt increasingly remorseful that Judge Craig treated his clients so harshly, particularly Pearl and Gertie. To try to rectify that wrong, that August he asked Governor DeForest Richards to pardon the women. In a letter accompanying his Petition for Pardon, Greenfield wrote:

> I believe that if a trial had been had before a jury a conviction could not have been secured, and the heavy sentence the court pronounced astonished me.
>
> I have received no other money than what the county paid me for defending these parties and am making this application because I believe the girls are unjustly confined.
>
> One of the girls [Gertie] is in an advanced state of pregnancy and is certainly entitled to your careful consideration. The other one is a young girl and [I] do not think the influence in the penitentiary would make her a better girl in the next two years.

Greenfield also expressed his concern that neither the penitentiary at Rawlins nor Laramie had facilities or accommodations to properly care for a prospective mother. Further, he pleaded that "your petitioner is anxious to gain a pardon before delivering her child, so that she may be home and with her folks at the time of her confinement, where she can receive the necessary care and treatment for herself and child." According to Dr. A.B. Hamilton, the prison physician, "I can say I have twice examined her & to the best of my belief & from all I can learn from her, I think she will come a mother about the last of November or the first of December."

Warden Fleck confirmed Gertie's condition during a follow-up visit to her cell. "I personally saw and talked with her," he reported to officials of the State Board of Charities and Reform, "and there is no doubt that she is in the condition claimed. She is abnormally large and . . . . her limbs are swelling." After consulting with the prison doctor, he concluded, too, that "she should be released as soon as possible fearing some accident should happen that might give rise to criticism in some quarters." Fleck added, "She has sufficient money to take her to Denver where she claims she has good friends who will care for her this winter." With a touch of compassion, he asked the Board to "Please allow me to give her such part of the clothing allowance of $15.00 in cash as she wants as she can purchase what she needs in Denver cheaper than I can get it here."

Supported by a recommendation from the Board's officials to release Gertie on humanitarian grounds, Governor Richards finally signed the pardon on August 26. Two days later, upon learning of the governor's action, Warden Fleck at the Laramie prison immediately freed Gertie and, per instructions, sent her on to Denver.

PEARL PROMISES TO BE PENITENT

In the meantime, attorney Greenfield continued to pursue a pardon on behalf of the second "sister." "Pearl Smith is a girl of tender years and believes that her confinement is unjust," he told the Governor. "She has always born a good reputation and is a peaceable quiet girl, honest and of good character, and," he added, "is anxious to gain her liberty."

Her husband, Claude Bowman, also aggressively sought her freedom by traveling by train to Cheyenne, where he met with Governor Richards at the State Capitol. Pardon Pearl, Bowman pleaded, and he promised to "take her to Kansas City, and give her a good home and try to make a good woman of her."

Impressed by the spouse's offer, and convinced by his review of the case that Pearl "was more of a giddy girl than a criminal," the governor sent the following note to Bowman, staying at the home of Pearl's parents in Denver:

> I have concluded to pardon your wife, Pearl Smith, who is now in the penitentiary, with the distinct understanding that you immediately go and get her and take her, either to Denver or better, to Kansas City, as you stated you would.
>
> If you will come by here and see me, I will have the pardon issued, so that you can take it up there and get her and take her away immediately.

With a copy of Governor Richards's December 17 pardon in hand, Bowman left the following day for Laramie. Where, upon Pearl's release from prison, they departed for Kansas City.

POSTSCRIPT

Just about a week before Governor Richards granted Pearl's freedom, Gertie died in Denver while giving birth to her child.

The infant's father fared a bit better. With the support of a new attorney, George E. Brimmer, convict James Martin submitted an Application for Pardon to Governor Richards's successor, Bryant B. Brooks.

Witnesses not only confirmed Martin's presence in the Club Saloon at the time of the thefts, but the staffs of victimized stores also attested that he did not commit the crimes for which he served time.

Murphy, released on September 20, 1906, after serving his full sentence—less 255 "good time" days—also proclaimed Martin's innocence. "The most that can be said of the Martin," Murphy said, "was that he was in company with . . . parties [Murphy and the Smith girls] while in Rawlins, but that the crime was committed without his knowledge and during his absence."

Finally, armed with that host of evidence, and sympathetic towards Martin's deteriorating health caused by chronic rheumatism, Governor Brooks mercifully pardoned him on December 12, 1906.

SOURCES CITED

The primary source documents used in developing this story may be found in the Carbon County District Court Criminal Case Files #492, #493, and #494; Governor DeForest Richards's Petitions and Pardons Files re Pearl and Gertie Smith; Governor Bryant B. Brooks's Petitions and Pardons File re James Martin, as well as Governors Richards's and Brooks's Letterbooks and Correspondence files for the periods, respectively, of January 29, 1901, July 18, 1902 and June-December 1906. These materials are on file at the Wyoming State Archives.

Perhaps the most descriptive information available concerning the protagonists' crimes may be found in local and regional newspapers, the *Cheyenne Daily Leader* and the *Rawlins Republican*, during the period from May 2, 1902 through May 21, 1906.

Additional sources included the Wyoming State Penitentiary Descriptive Reports of Convicts Received and Convicts Discharged or Removed, as well as Mug Shot Descriptions that provides detailed physical information concerning Pearl Smith (Prisoner #680), Gertie Miller (Prisoner #681), Joseph Murphy (Prisoner #682), and James Martin (Prisoner #683). Also, the correspondence of Governor DeForest Richards includes testimonials regarding Pearl's early life and character from her mother, friends, and previous employers.

Prison conditions that led to the transfer of the women from the State Penitentiary at Rawlins to the State's auxiliary prison in Laramie are explained in the May 29 and August 4, 1902, Wyoming State Penitentiary Commissioners' Meeting Minutes as well as the Board of Charities and Reform Minutes, 1891–1961, that are on file at the Wyoming State Archives.

Special insight regarding James's lack of participation in the crime for which the State imprisoned him comes from his friend Joseph Murphy's July 9, 1906, affidavit as found in Governor Bryant B. Brook's Petitions for Pardons Files.

Joe Nash's Rambler

IT SEEMED LIKE A simple transaction. He plunked down his September 6, 1903, Cosgriff Sheep Company paycheck, and she shared her charms. He claimed satisfaction for the moment. And she made a few quick, easy bucks. Only one problem: the husband believed his wife to be worth more than four dollars. So he rectified the situation by inking a couple of extra zeroes after the four and before the decimal.

Joseph F. and Emma Lenora Nash, a young Mormon couple, ran a sheep camp about fifty miles north of Rawlins for a Carbon County sheep company. Born in Utah, they each completed a fifth grade education and, apparently, subsequently lived temperate lives. It is not known where they met and married. What is sure, however, is that Emma "was formerly a belle in Provo, Utah" before her parents, Mr. and

Emma Lenora Nash (Inmate #780) shared herself with a sheepherder for his four-dollar paycheck. Later, she and her husband Joe hiked the value of her wares by penning in a greater amount on the check. When they fraudulently cashed the instrument, they earned stays in prison. (Wyoming Division of Cultural Resources)

Mrs. Henry Swabes moved to South Dakota. Joe's parents, "Jas." and Mrs. Nash, resided in Vernal, Utah.

In 1901, Joe and Emma moved east to Wyoming, where, for a time, they worked as cooks on sheep ranches in the southern part of Carbon County. As part of his work, Joe frequently spent several days at a time afield tending flocks. During one such extended stay, a herder by the name of Perfecto Macs showed up at the Nashes' home and the

Joe Nash (Inmate #781). (Wyoming Division of Cultural Resources)

Mexican took a shine to the pouty-lipped prostitute, whose catlike, "yellow" eyes observed him through her wire-rimmed glasses. At five feet, four and a half and 132 pounds, the dark-haired woman probably cut quite a figure.

Whether by accident or design, they soon compromised their respective moral values and satisfied their baser needs, his for sex and hers for money in the form of a check made payable by M. Winkleman for Macs's boss, Thomas A. Cosgriff. No stranger to illicit transactions, the sultry Emma had probably hoisted her skirt for a check or its cash equivalent on more than a few occasions. In fact, subsequent events suggest Emma's husband not only knew of his wife's indiscretions, but encouraged such enterprise.

When the twenty-six-year-old Joe returned to their cabin the following day and found that Emma had sold her sex for a pittance, they probably exchanged a few hot words regarding the value of her tarnished virtue. As a consequence, Joe bumped the total of Macs's note one hundred times to the munificent sum of four hundred dollars. "That's more like it!" Joe probably thought. Soon thereafter, Nash and his wife quit their camp and went to Rawlins, where they tried to pass the fraudulent check at J.W. Hugus & Co. But unlike Macs, the folks at the store refused the bargain. Continuing east, the Nashes arrived on September 17 in Cheyenne, where they hoped to bilk someone there. After purchasing a number of items at Samuel Beyman's secondhand store, they offered the altered check in payment to the owner. When Beyman examined the draft and found it lacked an endorsement, Emma tried to correct the matter. In the presence of the proprietor and her husband, she penned an "M"—for Macs—on the back of the note. When Beyman refused the initialed certificate, Joe compounded Emma's felony by grabbing her pen and completing her paying paramour's full name.

Although still probably suspicious, Beyman processed the check along with his other receipts. Several days later, however, officials of the First National Bank confirmed the store owner's suspicions when they pronounced it worthless. Upon notification of the crime, Sheriff Edwin J. Smalley quickly responded by arresting the Nashes and locking them away in the Laramie County Jail to await their fate.

Several weeks later, the county's District Attorney Walter R. Stoll indicted Joe and Emma on two counts: 1) "Feloniously and falsely contriving to damage and defraud the Cosgriff Sheep Company" and 2) attempting to "knowingly, alter, publish and pass as true and genuine" a fraudulent bank draft. Specifically, authorities charged the couple with forging, counterfeiting, and passing the First National Bank of Rawlins check "No. 4237" to Samuel Beyman. Not until the arraignment and preliminary trial on Monday morning, October 12, however, did they throw themselves on the mercy of the court and, without hesitation, plead "guilty" to both charges.

END OF THE TRAIL

Justice came swiftly. Having heard the evidence and their plaintive pleas, First Judicial District Court Judge Richard H. Scott pronounced their sentences:

> It is therefore considered, ordered and adjudged by the Court that the said defendants, Emma Lenora Nash and Joseph Nash, be imprisoned and confined in the penitentiary of the State of Wyoming, for the period of one year from this date, that during said confinement they shall be clothed, subsisted and treated in all respects in accordance with the rules and regulations governing that institution, and there be safely kept there until the term of their confinement shall have expired, or until they shall have been otherwise discharged according to the law.

Two days later, Deputy Sheriff Les Snow loaded Emma and Joe aboard the train and escorted them west to the

Wyoming State Penitentiary in Rawlins. Admitted, respectively, as inmates #780 and #781, the Nashes became the only married couple to serve time concurrently in that great, gray-stoned prison. Although there is no record that Emma either saw or talked to her husband during their incarceration, she at least had the company of Anna E. Trout and Viola Biggs, after authorities sentenced the mother-daughter duo to the women's ward the following March 24.

There in the Wyoming State Penitentiary, Emma and Joe remained in their respective cells until August 22, 1904, when Warden J.P. Hehn released the couple—each having been allowed fifty days' "good time"—"by reason of expiration of sentence."

Presumably, the contrite couple returned to Utah and, one hopes, resumed the moral, righteous, and upstanding lives of their youth and their faith.

SOURCES CITED

In addition to the Laramie County District Court Criminal Case File #4-97—containing the October 3, 1903, Information and Indictment and the October 12, 1903, sentencing paperwork, the Laramie County Sheriff's Prison Calendar (June 14, 1901-1905) and Wyoming State Penitentiary's Inmate Files #780 and #781 proved especially helpful in providing information about the Nashes' physical descriptions and characteristics.

Newspaper accounts of the crimes and the criminals' dispositions may be found in both the *Cheyenne Daily Leader* (October 3 and 13, 1903), the *Carbon County Journal* (August 27, 1904), and the *Rawlins Republican* (August 27, 1903, and August 31, 1904).

As the Stomach Turns

 TABLOID EDITORS SALIVATE over such sad little sagas. Talk show hosts, too, drool to probe the psyches of protagonists like these. In fact, this is the kind of story that seems to dominate much of today's news.

There is a deadbeat dad who refuses to support his spouse or pay their baby's medical bills. Also, we find a weak wife who won't, for whatever reason, leave her mother. And then the mother-in-law from hell arrives on the scene.

No, this is not a pretty tale. But it happened in Casper, Wyoming, in 1902.

THE WEDDING DAY

It all started well enough when the winsome, red-haired Viola wed John William Biggs that November 22. The couple seemed happy with their new life, but then times turned tough, and they moved in with the young bride's parents, Jno. M. and Anna E. Trout. Three siblings also still lived at home: two sisters, ages fourteen and eight, plus an eighteen-year-old brother. At first, things worked well as Annie treated her son-in-law "kindly." The forty-two-year-old matron even "loaned him furniture and did everything possible to make it pleasant for him and help him to get a start in life." At least, that is the story told by twenty-year-old Viola.

Unfortunately, as many who try such a familial arrangement will testify, the limited privacy soon took its toll. John yearned for a home of their own, but the five-foot, two-inch lass with eyes of blue demurred. She "refused to leave her mother."

Then the inevitable happened. Viola proclaimed her pregnancy and the Biggs's marital bliss almost immediately wore thin under the rasp of domestic disputes and bickering. By mid-May 1903, John called it quits and moved out of the Trouts' house. Regretting their split, Viola went to John and pleaded for him to come back, but he refused. "Married life," he claimed, "ain't what it is cracked up to be." Still anxious to make up, she joined him several months later in his room at the Grand Central Hotel. After a couple of nights together, however, he told her to go. He did not have enough money to pay her board, he said. Instead, he put her off by saying that "maybe" he would rent a house after the birth of their child.

Distraught, the pregnant Viola returned to her folks. That is when John told her that he'd changed his mind, did not want to raise their child, and encouraged her to "get rid" of it. When she refused, he told her physician, as well as

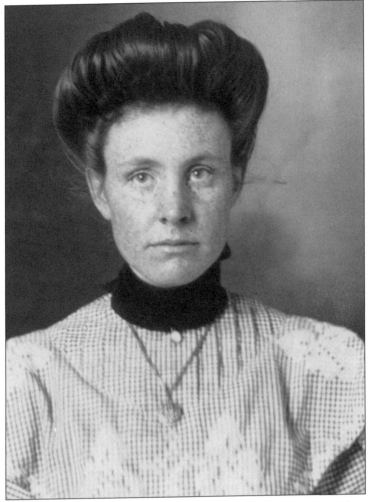

Viola Biggs (Inmate #817) and her mother Anna E. Trout found their way into prison on kidnaping charges when the couple conspired to abandon Viola's child—Anna's grandson—at the railway station in Denver, Colorado. (Wyoming Division of Cultural Resources)

folks at the store where Viola most frequently shopped, that he refused to be liable for any of her bills.

MARIETT'S BIRTH

On August 16, she gave birth to a boy, at first named Mariett Archer Biggs. Following the child's delivery, Viola repeatedly asked John to at least see his son, but, he said, he "did not want to be bothered with a baby." He refused, too, to take back his wife.

Viola's parents continued to support both her and the child, but the new mother found herself unable to leave her baby long enough to ply her skills as a stenographer, and the family larder came under stress. Instead, she helped her dressmaker mother by doing needlework. The struggle, however, became too much.

In one last try at reconciliation, Viola told John that unless he shared in Mariett's support she planned to put their boy up for adoption. Still he refused. So on the morning of September 10, as John looked on without protesting, the two women set off with the infant toward the Casper railway station. Annie, with the consent of her daughter, took the month-old Mariett south to Denver, where she planned to put him up for adoption. Unsatisfied, however, with Mrs. Trout's answers to their questions, foundling home officials refused to admit the child.

Still determined to unload her burden, Annie took the child the following day to the local Union Pacific depot. The station matron Sarah Thomas recalled later that, while she cleaned the ladies' waiting room, Annie entered and asked "if she could leave her baby in my care while she went up town to do some shopping." Thomas replied that "one could not very well shop at nighttime," then returned to her work. In the meantime, Annie penciled the following note on a sheet of coarse paper and pinned it to the baby's gown: "Please take baby to orphans' home. He was born August 16. His name is Leonard Trout." She then left the building to return via train to Casper.

"That evening," said Thomas, "I heard a baby crying, and looking about, saw that the wail came from a lonely bundle." The babe's face, she told a *Denver News* reporter, appeared:

> . . . so drawn and lined . . . that it wore the aspect of an adult. Its little frame is a bundle of bones; about the eyes are distinct crow's feet and the lines around the mouth and between the brows are as distinctly marked as if years of worry had imprinted them.

Continuing, Thomas said, "When I picked it up and I saw the note, read it and knew that the woman who had spoken to me fifteen minutes before was she who had left the baby." The child, "coarsely but cleanly dressed," added the depot employee, "wore a long dress of cotton flannel and was found wrapped in a gray woolen woman's cape." She also retrieved a small bundle containing a pair of shoes, two pairs of stockings, and two outfits of baby clothing near the infant.

Thomas immediately called the authorities, who took the baby to city hall, where they put him into the care of Mrs. Clark, a mother imprisoned in the jail there with an infant of her own. There, in her cell, she fed the wasted waif from her child's bottle before stowing the tot next to her babe for the night. During that first tenuous night, a few

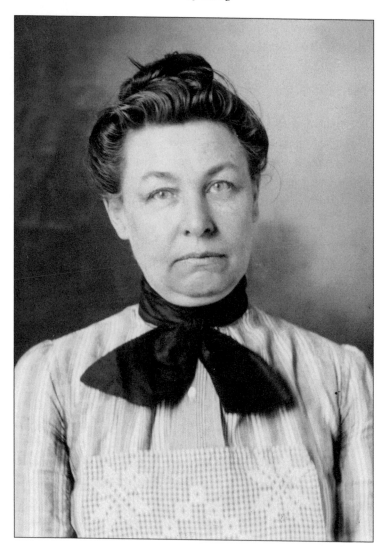

Anna E. Trout (Inmate #818). (Wyoming Division of Cultural Resources)

onlookers feared the tad might die. With Mrs. Clark's tender care and the aid of the city's physician, however, the abandoned baby so quickly improved that, the following day, officials at Denver orphan's home accepted the infant for care under the auspices of the local humane society.

The morning after leaving Mariett (Leonard) with her mother at the station, Viola encountered John at a local restaurant. Going to him, because she wanted to see him "awfully well," she tearfully lied to him that she sent their child away ... to Deadwood, South Dakota. She told John, that unless he took her back, he would never again see his son.

KIDNAPING CHARGED

Following extensive news coverage and a tentative identification of the child, Denver police notified their Casper counterparts about the incident. The Natrona County Attorney and Prosecutor John M. Hench immediately responded by going to Denver, where he helped confirm the baby's name and lineage. On September 23, John Biggs's mother, Martha Harris, followed and retrieved the child. It took nearly a week, however, before she returned the baby to Casper as she had some difficulty retrieving him from the orphanage.

Three weeks later (October 14), the irate father filed kidnaping charges against both his mother-in-law and his wife, whom the police arrested that same afternoon. They remained in Sheriff Frank K. Webb's custody until about nine o'clock that night when they secured bonds of five hundred dollars each before being released. In the meantime, John's mother petitioned the court for control of the baby.

Despite the Casper community's indignation over the affair and accompanying editorial attacks, supporters of Viola and Annie threatened Attorney Hench to "tend to his own business and let up on the kidnaping case." The barrister, however, refused to be intimidated. Instead, he responded stiffly that he "could generally be found at his office, where the latch string is always hanging out for friend or foe."

In the meantime, the preliminary trial of the State versus Annie and Viola convened at ten A.M. on Tuesday, October 27, but, because their attorney, Fred Hammond, claimed insufficient time to prepare his case, the judge agreed to delay their hearing.

When the case resumed the following November 11, a variety of witnesses came forth to confirm the identity of the child, who remained throughout the trial in the care of his paternal grandmother. "It seemed," according to those present, "to take great interest in its mother, whom it had not seen for several months." Fortunately, the boy's infancy spared him the nasty testimony that followed. John swore that even though the baby arrived "276 days after" their marriage, "his relations with Viola . . . before marriage were such that the child could be born before that date named and he would be the father." Although the prosecution refused to call Viola and her mother to the stand, the women planned to make John prove his fatherhood once the trial moved to district court. They even suggested that "they will even go so far to prove that he is not [the father], and they will prove who is."

When the Second Judicial District Court of Natrona County convened on Wednesday afternoon, February 3,

1904, in Casper, the mother and daughter pleaded innocent to the charges brought against them. It took eleven days, however, before the jury took their seats and their first witness, John's mother, stepped to the stand.

TRIED & SENTENCED

The wheels of justice ground on until 7:30 P.M. eight days later, when the foreman W.E. Tubbs declared, "We, the jury, duly empaneled and sworn to try the issue in the above entitled cause do find the defendants, Viola Biggs and Anna E. Trout, guilty in the manner and form as charged in the information [indictment]." Tubbs added a "recommendation of the court's clemency to the defendant, Viola Biggs." The verdict, according to the media, seemed "to meet with the approval of a great majority of the people of the town and county."

Frail Viola immediately broke down and wept bitterly as she pleaded unsuccessfully to Judge Charles E. Carpenter that he keep her from jail. Annie, however, took the decision stoically and with seeming contempt.

It took Judge Carpenter nearly five more days of study and soul searching, however, before he finally decided their sentences. By the morning of Tuesday, February 23, their demeanor had changed. Now Annie came into court leaning heavily upon the arm of her husband, Mr. Trout, while Viola walked "unattended with a firm step." That changed soon thereafter. After approaching the bench, the judge asked Viola, "Have you anything to say why sentence and judgment should not be pronounced upon you?"

"Well, sir," she replied, "I am not guilty. That is all I have to say."

After assuring all concerned that he did not relish the "most unpleasant duty," Judge Carpenter proceeded to pronounce judgment. Despite the fact that her husband "wholly failed to keep his marriage vows," the judge said he found Viola's abandonment of her own child so despicable that "an example must be made." Continuing, the judge said:

> It is ordered, considered, adjudged and decreed by the court, that you, the said VIOLA BIGGS, defendant, be remanded to the custody of the sheriff of Natrona County, State of Wyoming, and that within the time provided by law, the said sheriff of said county shall take you and deliver you to the warden, keeper, or other proper officer of the Wyoming State Penitentiary, situated at or near the city of Rawlins, in the County of Carbon, in the State of Wyoming, and that you, the said, VIOLA BIGGS, be therein imprisoned and confined for the period of one year in the said, Wyoming State Penitentiary, and that you be governed, clothed and subsisted, according to the rules and regulations of said institutions, and that you be adjudged to pay the costs of the action.

Viola returned to her seat at the defendant's table. The judge next instructed her mother to approach the bench.

"I am not guilty," Annie said in a soft, nearly inaudible, quivering voice.

The judge reminded her, prior to pronouncing sentence, that she "was of mature mind, and her judgment should have been better than that of her daughter's. She should have advised and influenced her daughter against the desertion of her child, but instead she encouraged her in the desertion of the helpless babe, and she even took it away and left it." For that unforgivable lapse of responsibility, Judge Carpenter sentenced her to eighteen months, six more than his charge to her daughter.

RETRIAL SOUGHT

Defense attorney Fred D. Hammond responded by quickly securing a delay in their delivery to the penitentiary until the Wyoming Supreme Court might rule for or against a new trial for the two women. In the meantime, Sheriff Webb whisked the guilty ladies off to jail. There, he confined them in a makeshift "ladies cell"—out of sight and sound of the male prisoners' cages—within an apartment across the hall from the sheriff's own living quarters.

Witnesses said later that Viola at first "gave vent to her feelings copiously, on account of her humiliation, but after a night's rest she became reconciled and bore up more bravely." Although Annie wept, she, too, seemed to become more philosophical about her fate.

The following Saturday morning, a bailiff brought the women back to the court. Attired in the same "very plain" clothing that she wore throughout her hearing, Annie showed the toll of that ordeal. Viola, on the other hand, "looked as bright and almost as free from care as she did during the trial." She wore "a modest red waist and plain black skirt," but instead of the "rich hat trimed with gorgeous white plumes, that she previously wore, she had thrown over her head a plain white fascinator [scarf]."

The heated debate by Hench and Hammond that followed kept the attention of both the court and the defendants until proceedings ended with a rap of the magistrate's gavel. The following Monday morning, Judge Carpenter announced that, although his sympathy "went out to the defendants on account of their sex," nothing convinced him to grant their attorney's motion for a new trial.

The following month turned their lives to hell after authorities moved the two women from their relatively comfortable quarters into a regular cell. There, separated only by a grid of strap-iron from male convicts, Viola and Annie found themselves sandwiched between felons "in such a state . . . they made it extremely obnoxious." Desperate under such conditions, the ladies begged to be moved. The authorities, too, wanted the women incarcerated elsewhere, because of "the crowded conditions of the jail." The court finally agreed to ship the "kidnapers" off to Cheyenne for lodging in the Laramie County Jail until the State Supreme Court might act upon their appeal.

Although their situation improved, attorney Hammond suggested his clients agree to go to the state penitentiary, because of the more comfortable accommodations there. Even if the supreme court ruled against them, he said, they would serve at least half of their sentences by the time the court reached its decision. Viola and her mother promptly agreed. The following Thursday, Sheriff Webb escorted the pair to the Union Pacific depot at the south end of Capitol Street where, with their guard, they boarded the westbound train to Rawlins. Several hours later, the trio disembarked and the lawman led his charges north up the hill to the penitentiary.

Once settled in their new quarters, they sent word to their family and asked them to send them a trunk of clothes. More garments followed from friends as the women seemed to settle into their new quarters. Some even reported that "One of the reasons they so strongly protested against going to the penitentiary after being convicted was the thought that their hair would be cut off." When that did not happen, their attitudes apparently improved immensely. During a subsequent visit to the penitentiary, Sheriff Webb said he found Viola and Annie there in the women's ward "comfortably situated, having a nice large room full of flowers, and as being contented."

SUPREME COURT APPEAL

Attorney Hammond, in the meantime, filed a petition with the Wyoming Supreme Court, alleging, among other things, that the district court verdict, contrary to evidence, violated the law and the instructions of Judge Carpenter.

Having reviewed the preliminary evidence of Hammond's charges, the State's Attorney General J.A. Van Orsdel agreed. In his words: "I am forced to the conclusion, after carefully reading the evidence in this case three times, and studying it in all its phases, that the evidence conclusively discloses that Biggs not only abandoned his wife in May prior to the birth of the child, but he notified the family physician that he would not be liable for any bills contracted by his wife, and also the Webel Mercantile Company to the same effect." In summary, he said that he failed "to find sufficient evidence against the women to sustain the judgment of the court."

After debating the case for roughly five months, the Wyoming Supreme Court justices outlined their findings.

1. To constitute the act of kidnaping, the removal of a child too young to be capable of objection must have been from the possession, actual or constructive, of the lawful custodian or against the will of someone authorized to object.

2. Where a husband abandoned his wife before the birth of his child, and thereafter did not live with, support, or in any way care for her, was not at any time in the custody or possession until after the mother with his knowledge had sent the child, when less than a month old, in charge of its grandmother to another state; Held, that the father had abandoned the sole custody of the child to the mother, and, further, by standing by without objection, when he knew the child was being carried off, he gave implied consent to its removal, and the mother and grandmother were not, therefore, guilty of the crime of kidnaping in so removing the child.

3. Under a statute giving the father the right of guardianship of a minor child in preference to the mother, it is the actual state of things, and not the existence of a mere legal relation, that is contemplated.

4. A mother and grandmother who removed a minor child, too young to object into another state are not guilty of kidnaping under the statute, where the father consented to such removal, though the latter may have been at the time in the actual custody of the child and entitled thereto.

Having expressed those opinions, Chief Justice Samuel T. Corn concluded on August 23 in a majority decision that the lower court, indeed, prosecuted Viola and Annie "in error." Further, he sent that opinion via letter to Warden J.P. Hehn at the Wyoming State Prison. Two days later, upon receipt of the Chief Justice's decision, the warden released the ladies "by reason of order by the Supreme Court" and sent them back to Casper, where he instructed officials there to hold the women in jail pending a new trial. That same day, however, District Court Judge Carpenter called from out of town to Sheriff Webb in Casper, ordering him to immediately release Viola and her mother. Authorities later dismissed all previous charges against the women.

In the absence of new evidence, all members of the Trout and Biggs families—including baby Mariett—promptly retreated into well-deserved anonymity.

SOURCES CITED

The most effective primary source documents used to tell this story may be found in the microfilm files (MA#8274) concerning Wyoming Supreme Court Case #2-446, *State of Wyoming v. Viola Biggs and Annie E. Trout.* Regrettably, for the sake of history, Natrona County District Court personnel are unable to find Criminal Case File #315 with its pertinent documents about the Biggs-Trout case. Officials at the Natrona County Sheriff's office also failed to locate the Prisoner Register and the Day Book for the general period the alleged kidnaping crime occurred.

Fortunately, however, the Wyoming State Penitentiary records regarding Inmates #817 and #818 Files—including their mug shots—provide a highly detailed physiological description of the women and provides significant insight about their interests and activities prior to prison.

Accounts of the alleged crime, as well as the women's subsequent trial, are described most graphically in such newspapers as the *Natrona County Tribune*, the *Wyoming Derrick*, the *Carbon County Journal*, and the *Laramie County Tribune*. For the best perspective of the entire affair, perhaps nothing summarizes the circumstances better than *Wyoming Reports: Cases Decided in the Supreme Court of Wyoming from April 25, 1904 to August 1, 1905*, "Biggs et al. v. State," Vol. 13, reported by Charles N. Potter (Laramie, WY: the *Laramie Republican* Office), April 1904.

When Hattie Met Harry

THERE ARE TWO versions of the story. His and hers. Regardless of which you choose, the ending is the same. Frank McKinney, aka "Harry H. Black," died a violent, untimely death in Thermopolis, Wyoming.

Best known by his alias, Black told witnesses from his deathbed the following:

Hattie telephoned me [shortly after nine P.M. on Thursday, September 14, 1905] at the Barr & Woods saloon to meet her at 11 o'clock near the stone house [brothel]; I went there, but did not see her, and then returned to the saloon; shortly after she came to the window and called me out; she asked me to walk up the street with her; then said, "Let us go round the back way;" she said she was sick, and asked me for money; I gave her $5.00; she said that during this walk there was no quarrel between us; when we crossed the street, near the barn, I said, I had to go back to the saloon, and she said she would walk back a little ways with me; when we had walked about twenty steps, she reached behind me and shot me; I turned part way round, and she shot me again in the face; I then turned and ran toward the saloon.

The petite and darkly attractive Hattie LaPierre remembered that night differently. Her attorney told it this way:

The said Black came to the affiant's room and took her by force on the street and after they had gone some distance from the house [at the corner of Mondell and 6th Streets] the said Black clenched his fist and reached for what affiant supposed was his gun and says, "I will kill you and will kill you now," using vile and abusive language; whereupon affiant believing that she was going to be shot . . . by Black, pulled a [.38-caliber] gun and shot the said Black."

Mortally wounded, Black staggered from the corner near Jim Allen's livery barn and ran haltingly three blocks toward the main part of town. From the Barr and Woods saloon, City Marshal William B. Methany heard Black's cries. Arising from the table where he sat, the lawman stepped to the door, then ran north up the unpaved street. "I saw a party coming down," Methany said. As Black approached the corner of Fifth and Arapaho, Methany recalled the following scene:

He cried out again and just at the time the hack drove round the corner, and I thought he was hollowing at the hack, wanting to get in, and as the hack kept coming on, and so did he, and when he got about half way across the street I saw that it was Black; but he did not hollow any more, and when he came into the light where I was standing in front of Barr and Woods saloon, he says, "that damned son of a bitch shot me twice; get the doctor;" and then he went on inside and I helped him to the door.

As Black collapsed to the floor, saloon customers Elmer Woods and Ed Fetters noticed he had a "little wound in the chin." After removing his coat and vest, they found he also had "a little blood in the back of his shirt." The men immediately picked Black up and carried him across the street to his room, where Dr. James R. Richards attended his injuries. Due to Black's poor condition, however, the doctor failed to find and remove the bullet buried deeply in the victim's back. Considering Black's chance "was about even for and against his recover," the physician decided only to wash and dress the wounds and hope for the best.

THE MARSHAL APPREHENDS HATTIE

Shortly thereafter—about 11:30 P.M.—Marshal Methany saw Hattie going down the street toward the saloon. Walking up to her, he asked for her gun, but she said she "had throwed it over into the yard." She then asked about Harry's status. When Methany told her that her bad man still breathed, she lamented that she "loved that man better than any man she ever saw," even though she knew he gave "money to another woman."

Then, perhaps realizing his own hunger, the marshal asked Hattie if she'd had supper. After learning that, despite the late hour, she had missed her meal, the lawman took her back to the Stone House, where her "landlady" fed them before he locked Hattie up in the city's jail.

During the long night that followed, W.S. "Scott" Briggs, who served as Black's "night nurse," said his patient spoke only once in his presence. When Scott suggested that he "had a close shave," Black responded, "Yes. The dam bitch was a good shot." A.R. Hagar remembered that as he, too, sat with Black the night following the shooting, the mortally wounded man acknowledged the inevitability of what happened. "It was one of the two of us sooner or later," he murmured.

The following day, while Black's deepest wound slowly drained his life's blood into the cavern of his body, Marshal Methany turned Hattie over to Deputy Sheriff Armstrong. She remained, however, only briefly in his custody. County Attorney and Prosecutor James S. Vidal directed that she be taken south to Lander, the seat of Fremont County, to be held in county jail there "awaiting the results of Black's injuries." They did not wait long. After languishing for nearly five days, Black died at two on Tuesday morning, September 19.

THEIR LONG ROAD ENDED IN THERMOPOLIS

Despite the disparities in the respective stories from Harry and Hattie, a clear chain of events preceded his death.

Hattie LaPierre (Inmate #965), according to some accounts, figuratively shot herself in the foot when she, literally, fired two lead slugs into the body of Frank McKinney, alias "Harry H. Black," who forced her into prostitution to help support his drinking and gambling. (Wyoming Division of Cultural Resources)

The Louisiana-born, twenty-year-old Hattie had met Harry about six months earlier. His dark hair, dark eyes, and "kinda-a dark" complexion quickly won her heart. He even convinced her to quit her job as a milliner and accompany him north to Wyoming, where he said they would marry.

In addition to his good looks and "powerful" physique, Hattie also found attractive the aura of danger about him. That mystique hid a history that soon haunted her. She learned, for example, that, in addition to being a "tin horn gambler," he "was a morphine and opium fiend and adicted to the liquor habit." Worse, Harry told her, he killed a woman before fleeing to Canada. Almost as an afterthought, he also admitted being a "fugitive from justice" for killing two men, one in New Mexico and another in Colorado. For the latter crime, Pueblo authorities held him in custody "for a long time charged with murder, but they never made a case against him." He said he also served a term in an undisclosed penitentiary for some other crime.

Shortly after arriving in Lander, Wyoming, about the last week of August 1905, the couple checked into a hotel as "H.H. Black and wife." During those days together, Hattie recalled, he "made gun plays and prided himself on being a bad man."

He also installed her in a house of prostitution while threatening to kill her unless she stayed there and helped support him. When he needed money—a regular occurrence—and she refused to share her earnings, he either stole them or beat her unmercifully and threatened her life until she coughed them up. And he needed all available financial help, because he gambled often, but not well. Mean and jealous, he also clubbed Hattie with his gun and fists when other men showed more than casual interest in his woman. Although his visciousness drove her to try to escape, her every attempt only brought more violence. During that summer, according to F.C. Lewis, a witness at her trial:

> Black, who had had some differences with . . . Hattie . . . disguised himself so that he would not be known to any one, when affiant by accident knew him and asked . . . Black where he was going; in reply to which . . . Black stated that he was going to lay for that D-S- of a B, meaning Hattie LaPierre; that he was during this time threatening the life of . . . Hattie.

Another witness, R.H. Earl, who knew Hattie and Harry, said he saw Black strike and beat Hattie as well as threaten to kill her. "From her action and what he knew of the circumstances," Earl said, he knew that Hattie "was in great fear of . . . Black at all times."

Finally fed up with their constant fighting, the "madam" forced Hattie to leave. They left Lander and traveled north to Thermopolis, the site of Wyoming's famed hot springs. There, Harry arranged for Hattie to go to work in the infamous Stone House, while he took an upstairs room with a male acquaintance, J.M. Mott, in nearby Cover's Saloon.

HARRY SHOT HATTIE

Mott later recalled that eight days before Hattie shot Harry she came to their room, her eyes swollen and bruised from Black's fists. She said she wanted one of her belongings from Black's trunk. Her lover-pimp, in the most "abusive and vulgar" language, refused her request. "Harry," she asked, "what makes you talk that way to me; what have I done for you to talk and treat me so?" According to Mott, the couple left the room

> . . . by way of a side door and immediately on the outside of the door the two parties had a conversation which affiant could hear, that during said conversation the said Black stated to the said Hattie . . . that she had better be careful and not get him started because she knew what she would get if he got started.

After escorting Hattie outside the building, Black returned to the room, where he got his gun and asked Mott for five dollars stating "he was going out and that there would be something doing."

Within the hour, Black shot "a hole . . . in one side" of Hattie's toe. Harry admitted firing the slug, but innocently called the wounding a mishap. According to his account, when he "went to put the hammer down on the gun . . . it slipped out from under his thumb and went off." Then, when Hattie, too, swore "it was an accident," no criminal charges resulted. Dr. H.L. Callaway simply treated her wound. In fact, all seemed forgotten—for the moment. Later that day, Black told Mott he "made a mistake, that he did not aim to shoot her where it would not count." Mott understood from that remark that Black meant to kill Hattie, because he also had "a married woman on the string."

THE POSTMORTEM EXAMINATION

The Tuesday Black died, coroner John A. Thompson initiated an inquest for which he swore Fred E. Winchester,

Paul Berg, and L.W. Goddard as jurors. That afternoon, the jury reviewed the body as Hagar, Methany, and Briggs testified regarding their evidence. The inquest continued until four. Because Doctor Richards did not complete his postmortem examination, the coroner rescheduled the hearing until eight P.M. the following evening, when the physician testified as to the following cause for Black's death:

> ...a .38 caliber mushroom bullet had penetrated the 11th rib just to the left of the spinal column, tearing through the right lung and lodging between the 6th and 7th ribs on the far right side, causing a wound that was necessarily fatal. The other bullet had drilled through the jaw bone just to the left of the point of the chin and lodged in the right side of the throat.

Although the physician's vivid description of that autopsy may have caused some of the more delicate women to choke back queasiness caused by late dinners, he seemed oblivious to their discomfort. Continuing, he added that:

> On opening the chest, I removed about three quarts of blood from the chest cavity. I discovered that one bullet had broken the 11th rib about one inch from the spine (to the right of the spine) and passed through the right lung imbedding itself in the chest wall between the 6th and 7th ribs two inches to the right of the right nipple line; in passing through the lung the bullet cut some of the branches of the pulmonary artery which was sufficient to cause death.

That same Wednesday afternoon, Rev. J.H. Gillespie accepted the body over which he conducted a funeral and laid it to rest "on the hill" per Black's last request. Later, while going through Black's personal effects, which included letters from his sister, Essie, of Galena, Kansas, authorities learned his true name: Frank McKinney.

CRIMINAL CHARGES FILED

Not until a week later did County Attorney and Prosecutor James S. Vidal file a criminal complaint against Hattie in the court of Justice of the Peace Charles Adams. Vidal charged that she "wilfully, unlawfully, feloniously, purposely and with premeditated malice, did kill and murder one Harry Black." That same day, Justice Allen signed a Criminal Warrant that ordered Sheriff Charles Stough "to apprehend the said Hattie LaPierre, the defendant and bring her before me to be dealt with according to the law." At the same time, he summoned Hagar, Methany, and Doctor Richards—among others—to testify at the October 6 preliminary hearing.

Three days later, Sheriff Stough delivered the defendant to Justice Allen's court. Having advised Hattie and her attorney of her rights, he told them that "further proceedings . . . is postponed and adjourned to the hour of nine o'clock in the forenoon the 6th day of October, 1905." In the meantime, he remanded her without bail to county jail.

When court convened at the appointed date and time, Justice Allen heard the various legal arguments before ruling that Hattie be charged with "murder in the second degree." Then, after setting her bail at five thousand dollars, he declared that she be held and tried at the next term of the District Court of the Second Judicial District. Unable to post bond, however, she remained in county jail.

Seeking to fortify her defense, Hattie brought in a new legal team—Stone & Winslow—whom she hoped would win her release. As the respective attorneys maneuvered in preparation for the forthcoming district court trial, prosecutor Vidal, assisted by D.A. Preston, initiated his indictment. The December 1 document alleged Hattie "did unlawfully, feloniously, purposefully and maliciously, but without premeditation, kill and murder one Harry Black" to which she pleaded "not guilty."

When district court failed to convene as planned on Monday morning, December 11, because Judge Charles E. Carpenter "was unavoidably delayed on his way to Lander," Clerk of Court Ben Sheldon immediately ordered a recess until nine A.M. the following Tuesday. Unfortunately for Hattie, the reprieve did not change the results: Judge Carpenter charged her with the crime as outlined in the indictment. Again she denied her guilt. Not until Friday, December 22, however, did Foreman Peter T. Peralta of Lander, deliver a verdict on behalf of the all-male jury: "We, the jury duly impaneled and sworn to try the issues in the above entitled cause, do find the defendant Hattie LaPierre guilty of the crime of manslaughter as charged in the information, and recommend her to the leniency of the court." Judge Carpenter showed little mercy during the subsequent sentencing proceedings as he condemned the former "belle du Thermopolis' demi-monde" to be imprisoned for three years in the State Penitentiary at Rawlins. According to a newspaper report of the trial:

Judge Carpenter is apparently determined to discourage crime by making an example of the criminals. In the Hattie LaPierre murder case from Thermopolis he gave the woman a term of three years, although she was only found guilty of manslaughter . . . There was an uncommonly heavy docket, both civil and criminal, and the judge evidently thinks the most effective way to deter others from committing crime is to inflict severe punishment on those who are found guilty. County Attorney Vidal is living up to the reputation he made while occupying the same place before—that of letting no guilty man escape.

In a related newspaper editorial, Hattie's character and crime came under attack:

The LaPierre crime should teach the young people that no immunity is to be expected from the courts on account of sex or condition in life to the naturally im- moral element. A man who beats, abuses and maltreats a woman, perhaps deserves to be killed by the woman and if the woman herself if without reproach juries might take a different view of such cases.

The Appeals Process

After Sheriff Stough delivered Hattie to the State Peni- tentiary on January 7, 1905, it took her little time to settle into her new quarters. Apparently displeased with her legal team's inability to get her a new trial, she hired still another attorney, L.E. Armstrong, to plead her case. He quickly sent several petitions on her behalf to the Wyoming Board of Pardons. The documents, signed by more than two hundred petitioners, including nine of the twelve original district court jurors, said in part:

Your petitioners have learned, since the sentence has been pronounced upon the said HATTIE . . . a large amount of additional evidence which in a measure would justify the act of the said HATTIE . . . It appears that the said Black made numberless threats to take the life of the said HATTIE . . . and that on a number of ocassion did beat and maltreat her. That evidence will accompany this petition which shows that the said Black on different ocassions shot, and in at least two incidents has killed his victim. That the said Black stated when he shot the prisoner that his intentions were to kill her. That the said Black was an opium and morphine fiend and addicted to the liquor habit, all of which had a tendency to increase the vicious and cruel conduct towards the prisoner.

That on account of your petition having become acquainted with these facts in the case they believe that the imprisonment of the said HATTIE . . . is unjust, and that the ends of justice will in no way be violated in the exercise of executive clemency and in the granting of a pardon to the said HATTIE LAPIERRE.

WHEREFORE, your petitioners respectfully pray, the promises being considered, that the Board of Pardons will reccommend to his Excellency the exercise of his executive clemency and that he grant the said HATTIE LAPIERRE a pardon and a full release from the State Penitentiary.

Attorney Armstrong also sent letters to the rest of the jurors who heard Hattie's case so that they, too, had the additional uncovered evidence regarding Harry's sordid past and character. To facilitate the process, he also enclosed copies of the following form letter, which he asked them to sign and send along to the State Board of Pardons:

> Gentlemen:-I desire to state that I was one of the jurors in the case of the state of Wyoming vs. Hattie LaPierre, which Defendant was tried and convicted of Manslaughter in January, 1906, in the District Court of Fremont County, Wyoming. Since the conviction I have become acquainted with a large amount of evidence and facts connected with the man Black, whom defendant shot, which leads me to believe that the reasonable and honest fears, herself, not being the aggressor, she would be justified in the shooting, and you should acquit her.

Attorney Armstrong, in pleading her case, told the jurors that Hattie "is not in the best of health; she is alone, as there are no women in the penitentiary and her service there is in solitude." He said he believed that Hattie "did the community a good when she shot the man she killed and I believe also that if these and a great many other facts could have been produced had been shown in the evidence at the time, that the girl would have been acquitted."

When Fremont County Attorney Vidal learned of Armstrong's machinations and, in particular, that he provided a form letter to Hattie's jurors and encouraged them to sign and send the correspondence to the Board of Pardons, Vidal blew his stack. To help ensure the Board learned of Armstrong's antics, he advised its members:

> It has come to me notice that the parties seeking this pardon have in an underhanded manner resorted to

most disreputable and fraudulent methods of obtaining the signatures of jurors and other person to the Application-a sample of which is Attorney L.E. Armstrong's letter to the jurors and his prepared letters for the jurors to sign.

Apparently the members of the State Board of Pardons found nothing seriously wrong with Armstrong's lobbying tactics, because the following July 10, they recommended to Governor Brooks that he cut Hattie's sentence to fifteen months. The governor signed the commutation the following day and sent it that afternoon to Warden J.P. Hehn for his immediate action. With the sixty-five days' "good time" she earned, her sentence expired and she found freedom on January 29, 1907, never to be seen again . . . at least not in Wyoming.

Sources Cited

Unquestionably, the most authoritative file containing the facts surrounding the crime can be found in the Fremont County District Court Criminal Case file #376 and its related documents, plus preliminary court documents found in the Fremont County Justice of the Peace Docket Book, for the period February 26, 1885 to July 13, 1906 (p. 274), and the September 20, 1905, Inquest of Harry Black. Additional details regarding the case—most specifically the shooting—are included in such newspaper accounts as those found in the *Thermopolis Record, Wind River Mountaineer,* and the *Lander Clipper* during the period of September 16, 1905 through July 2, 1906.

A good understanding of the procedures that won Hattie's early release from prison may be gained, too, through the study of Petition and Pardon Records during Governor Bryant B. Brooks' term as well as through the review of correspondence contained in his personal files and letterbooks on file at the Wyoming State Archives.

Shame on the Shadows

THE SHADOW OF A great odd-shaped beast danced eerily on the wall as the couple bucked and heaved on the sweat-stained spread. Then it stopped as quickly as it started. No tender words. No signs of love. The weathered woman simply rolled from the bunk, shook the skirt from her pale thighs, and left the candlelit crib.

After a whispered exchange in the adjoining chamber, she returned to the Japanese gentleman in her bedroom. Picking up a cigarette, she leaned toward a taper. The harsh candle's light bleached her cheeks and made her hard features grotesque. Suddenly, a puff from her pursed lips snuffed the light. A rush of feet followed as toughs threw Tohichi Watanabe to the floor. As fingers probed his pockets and plucked his wealth, the wily man from the Far East

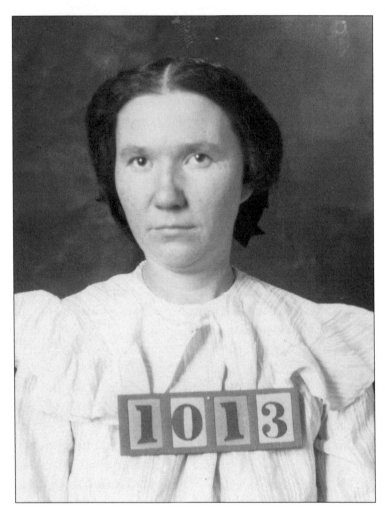

Dolly Brady (Inmate #1013), with her brothel goons, Art Cordieu and W.H. Bond, earned extended stays in the Wyoming State Penitentiary for robbing a wealthy Japanese customer. (Wyoming Division of Cultural Resources)

squirreled his diamond ring in his mouth and grabbed a loose garment before strong hands threw him into the street.

Regaining his composure, he soon found policemen C.H. Edwards and Thomas Holland, to whom he told his story. Together, they returned to Dolly Brady's brothel at 615 West 18th Street in Cheyenne. Unaware that Watanabe had taken a piece of her clothing when her thugs tossed him out her door, Dolly immediately claimed the item when the constables showed it to her. Having confirmed, in part, the victim's allegations, a search of the premises by the lawmen led to the silver coins from Watanabe's pocketbook cached beneath Dolly's stove. They also turned up the victim's tie and stick pin. Armed with that evidence, the police arrested the twenty-eight-year-old trollop and her compatriots, U.S. Army Private Arthur Cordieu and William H. Bond, before taking them to the city jail. They subsequently also found Watanabe's gold watch and chain in Cordieu's possession.

SHE COULDN'T BREAK HIS BILL

Watanabe's problems started earlier that Wednesday evening of March 21, 1906, when he crossed Dolly's stoop with a ten-dollar note. Unable to make change, the prostitute sent Bond out to break the bill. When he returned, Dolly kept five dollars for herself and returned the change to her customer before they consummated their relationship. That arrangement later led to the theft that landed Dolly and her duo in the pokey.

The following morning, Constable Keeley brought the defendants before Justice of the Peace A.E. Trump. According to charges filed against the trio, they did forcibly and feloniously make an assault . . . and did then and there . . . by violence and by putting in fear, take from the person of Tohichi Watanabe one gold watch ($35.00), one gold chain ($28.00), one gold locket ($15.00), one tie pin ($2.00), one match box (45-cents), one neck tie (50-cents), five $20.00 gold pieces ($100.00), two $10.00 gold pieces ($20.00), seven silver dollars ($7.00), one silver half dollar (50-cents), three 25-cent pieces (75-cents), all of said . . . good and lawful money of the United States of the America, and all of the said goods, chattels and personal property of the value of $219.20.

Dolly's attorney, M.J. Barry, claiming he lacked sufficient time to study the evidence, asked the court for a delay. Justice Trump agreed and rescheduled the hearing of Dolly's case until ten A.M. on following Saturday (March 24).

The dark-haired and mustachioed Bond next went to the bench and pled "not guilty." Prosecution witnesses, including Thisi Watanabe, another Japanese gentleman with the same last name as the accused, as well as interpreter Sunoe Inouye, and officers Edwards and Hollard, stepped forward. After the thirty-two-year-old Bond spoke on his own behalf, Justice Trump bound him over to the Third Judicial District Court of Laramie County.

The blond-haired, pale-eyed Cordieu, the Eleventh Infantry, Company C soldier who next went before Justice Trump, readily seemed to accept his fate, because, without hesitation, he simply pled "guilty." Since neither man posted the required seven-hundred-dollar bond, a bailiff took the nineteen-year-old soldier and the chicken-breasted Canadian

Art Cordieu (Inmate #1009) (Wyoming Division of Cultural Resources)

machinist to county jail, where they awaited further hearings of their cases.

Two days later, Dolly returned to the justice court where, again, Holland, Edwards, and Watanabe—with Inouye's help—told their stories. Although attorney Barry brought in several other defense witnesses to join Dolly in speaking on her behalf, he did not gain her release. And so, when she did not post her seven-hundred-dollar bond, the police also took her to the county jail to await her trial in District Court. After more than a month's delay, Laramie County Attorney and Prosecutor William B. Ross filed his indictment against Dolly and her criminal cronies, Bond and Cordieu. In the vernacular of their time, the authorities charged them with holding up and robbing Mr. Watanabe, a "Jap," during his visit from Rock Springs. Not until June 6, however, did Sheriff Smalley's deputy L.E. Snow serve subpoenas to the appropriate witnesses.

Finally, on Wednesday morning, June 14, the District Court trial got underway. In an unusual twist, Cordieu refused to testify when placed on the stand "on the ground that he would incriminate himself." He made that claim in spite of the fact that he previously "acknowledged his guilt in the Justice's court and indicated his intention of pleading guilty in the district court." To eliminate this objection, Judge Roderick N. Matson suspended Dolly's case until he tried Cordieu on the charge of robbing Watanabe, an allegation to which, after reflection, he again pleaded guilty.

With that settled, Dolly's trial immediately resumed with Cordieu being brought back to the stand. To every question regarding the robbery, however, he said only that "I do not remember."

Undoubtedly piqued by Cordieu's obstinate stonewalling, Judge Matson pressed for the respective attorneys to make their closing arguments that evening. The jurors apparently also grew impatient, because they reached their decision in no more than half an hour. Dolly broke down when the Clerk of the Court read the guilty verdicts before the bailiff led the couple back to their cells.

Attorney W.P. Carroll attempted to defend Bond the following day when the judge tried him for the same charges as those faced by Dolly and Cordieu. Unfortunately for the defense team, the prosecutor introduced evidence that:

> . . . certain correspondence alleged to have been written
> by the defendant to one Dolly Brady in which letter

purported to contain a confession or admission on the part of said Bond to the effect that he was one of the three persons who robbed and assisted in robbing one Watanabe of money and other valuables.

Faced with that bombshell, Bond fared no better than his cohorts in crime as the jury also found him guilty of robbery "in the manner and form as charged in the information."

Languishing in their respective jail cells, they went back before Judge Matson on Tuesday, December 4, for sentencing. Few found the results surprising. Dolly and Cordieu earned sentences of two years each in the state penitentiary at Rawlins while Bond, on whom the constables found most of the loot, received three years and six months at that same location.

THE SOILED DOVE FEATHERS HER NEST

On Wednesday morning (the following day), Deputy Sheriff Snow escorted the three convicted criminals to the Union Pacific depot at the south end of Capitol Street, where they boarded the westbound train to Rawlins. Arriving at the Wyoming State Penitentiary that same evening, they underwent processing along with several other prisoners before being led to their respective cells. As Bond and Cordieu found new homes in the prison's A Block, a guard took Dolly, now known as Convict #1013, to the third floor women's ward. She found little consolation in the fact that Hattie LaPierre, who had arrived about six months earlier, sat in an adjoining cell. Although they probably had little more in common than their vocations, each had someone with whom to talk until Hattie left prison the following January.

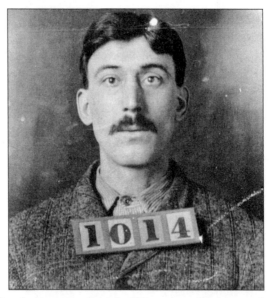

W.H. Bond (Inmate #1014) (Wyoming Division of Cultural Resources)

Roughly three months later, April 2, 1907, Dolly received another surprise. Gerty Brown, a sinning "sister" from Cheyenne, entered the ward as "Convict #1080." Although authorities also arrested and convicted Gerty of robbery, she gained release a month before Dolly.

PLEA FOR A PARDON

Whether moved by chivalry, a guilty conscience, or a not-so-subtle suggestion by strong-willed Dolly, Bond wrote to Wyoming's Governor Bryant B. Brooks:

> ... she [Dolly] is about to put in an application for an pardon   I wish to say that you will be entending

executive clemency towards one who justly deserves the same at your hands for your excellency she is innocent of the charge for which she is now being punished. Your excellency pardon this woman and by doing so you will simply be doing your duty for I swear by all I hold sacred that she is innocent . . . If I had been pirmitted to take the stand as an witness in her behalf she would never have come to this place I was prevented from doing so by the district attorney Ross   I wish to say in conclusion that Dolly Brady was almost an entire stranger that I never stopped overnight or had at any time intercourse with her or any inmates of her house   that I wrote to you to let you know that the woman is innocent therefore she should be granted her freedom   I am willing to swear that this is an true statement and as I hope for pardon in the beyond when I stand before the all wise judge I will say then as I say now that this is true She may be bad but she is not guilty of the crime for which she is here for   I hope your excellence will consider this matter and grant her petition is the wish of Wm. H. Bond.

About two weeks later, Dolly, too, made contact with the governor. Rather than write directly to Wyoming's chief executive, she chose instead to communicate, via the new Laramie County Attorney and Prosecutor Clyde M. Watts and the State Board of Pardons, that she wanted Governor Brooks to "either grant her a pardon or . . . commute her sentence to a shorter one." In pleading her case, Dolly acknowledged, in the third person:

she was the keeper of a bawdy-house in Cheyenne in which, or near which the crime is said to have been committed . . . it was the resort of many evil-minded men, and, like all such places, a place where men in their cups abandon themselves to recklessness; confessedly many depredations are committed in such a place . . . while her morals have been lax, she has always avoided such crimes as larceny and robbery for which she has had many opportunities.

Despite that admittedly soiled history, she asked that her "long and honest residence" be given weight in considering her call for clemency. But her pleas fell on deaf ears. After reviewing her application for pardon, as well as the related correspondence, the State Board of Pardons members concluded at their July 3, 1907, meeting that her pardon request be denied. The governor concurred.

POSTSCRIPT

Like so many of her predecessors who passed through the state penal system, Dolly quietly served the rest of her time before being discharged—with four months' "good time"—on March 26, 1908, by reasons of "expiration of sentence." Cordieu gained his release roughly two weeks earlier.

Bond, perhaps, fared the best of the three. Despite the fact that the judge sentenced him to three and a half years in the pen, Governor Brooks apparently succumbed to the felon's pleas for clemency, because he ruled that Bond and Dolly be released on the same date.

SOURCES CITED

As with many of the other stories in this book, the most important primary sources needed to reconstruct the crimes and their consequences came from district court criminal case files and penitentiary inmate records. Specifically, Laramie County Third District Criminal Case File #4-170 contains the witnesses' testimonies while mug shots and folders pertaining to Convicts #1009, #1013, and #1014, respectively, provided physical details about Cordieu, Brady, and Bond. And of course, the following newspapers offer the most colorful accounts of the characters and the impact of their actions upon the community: the *Cheyenne Daily Leader* and the *Wyoming State Tribune*.

Information contained in Cheyenne's Justice of the Peace A.E. Trump's docket also proved helpful by providing some of the more mundane details about the crimes and names, plus titles, of the city lawmen who responded.

Lastly, Governor Brooks's correspondence files and letterbooks, on file at the Wyoming State Archives, contain a variety of personalized pleas from the protagonists as well as from friends and acquaintances, who sought the release of this trio.

Scratch If It Itches

SO VERY LITTLE IS known about the petite, ebony Gertrude Brown that, in the dim light of time, the twenty-year-old widow and her baby boy barely cast shadows. But in her day, coaxed by cocaine, "Gerty" hopped like a flea from one misdeed to another until authorities in Cheyenne, Wyoming, decided to scratch her from the thin skin of their polite society. This they did, and well, on April 1, 1907.

The long, troubled trip, which eventually took Gertrude Brown into the Wyoming State Penitentiary in Rawlins, started with a single stride. It began August 12, 1906, when she got caught up in the annual Frontier Day "Wild West" festivities and local constables Warlaumont and Scholes arrested her for causing a "disturbance." Although Justice of the Peace A.E. Trump quickly discharged her without forcing

Gerty Brown (Inmate #1080) proved to be such a flea on the hide of Cheyenne's polite society that authorities there solved their problem by scratching her off the street and into a cell at the state's pen in Rawlins. (Wyoming Division of Cultural Resources)

her to serve time or pay a fine, that event seemed to serve as her first step on the slippery slope toward a life of crime.

Nine days later, Gerty again found herself in trouble. Although details are sketchy, Constable Keeley arrested her this time and took her to court, where Laramie County and Prosecuting Attorney William B. Ross charged that she stole:

> . . . three five dollar bills of the value of $15.00, one silver dollar of the value of one dollar, and 25-cents of the value of 25-cents and all of the value of $16.25 of the goods chattel and personal property of one Michael Luchi.

She tried to defend herself, but, in the face of more convincing testimony by her victim as well as Monto Vanto and A.H. Edwards, she failed to convince Justice Trump of her innocence. Unable to pay the fine of sixty dollars and costs, the bailiff took her to the Laramie County Jail the same day as her conviction (August 23) to serve ninety days in the slammer.

SHE FAILED TO LEARN HER LESSON

Did she learn her lesson? No such luck. Four months after she stepped from her cell, Constable T.A. Cosotto again took her into custody and delivered her before the bench of Justice W.F. Pagett. At ten o'clock in the morning on March 28, she found herself facing burglary charges. Specifically, the new Laramie County prosecutor Clyde M. Watts claimed that, two days earlier, she had stolen a five-dollar silk kimono and a Japanese jewelry box of equal value from Annie Page. Annie, like Gerty, helped earn her keep by "watching the ceiling" in a house of ill repute in Cheyenne's West End red-light district. Faced with overwhelming evidence, plus convincing testimony by the prosecutor's witnesses, Gerty accepted the path of least resistance by pleading guilty. Ordinarily, such an offense qualified as petit larceny, but because the court convicted her previously for that crime, the crime automatically became a grand larceny offense that First Judicial District Court Judge Roderick N. Watson tried only three days later.

Although entitled by right to a court-appointed counsel, Gerty deferred. So again, after a quick review of the allegations and evidence, she pled guilty to the charges as described in the indictment. Judge Watson needed little time before settling upon her sentence:

> It is . . . considered, ordered and adjudged by the court, that the said defendant, Gerty Brown, be imprisoned and confined . . . for a period of one year.

T.J. Fisher, Clerk of the District Court, immediately certified a copy of Judge Watson's sentence authorizing her transportation and confinement at the Wyoming State Penitentiary.

A JOURNEY WEST

Sheriff Smalley promptly returned Gerty to her cell in the county jail. The next morning they began their journey west to Rawlins. After she was processed as "Convict #1080," a guard escorted Gerty up the metal steps to her cell on the third floor of the main administration building. There she found a familiar face when she entered the women's ward—Dolly Brady, who lived and did her "business" next door to Gerty in Cheyenne. Dolly may have welcomed the company because she had served time there alone since Hattie LaPierre had left roughly two months earlier.

On February 29, 1908, Gerty, her sentence expired—thanks to one month's "good time" granted by Warden Fred Hillenbrand—watched quietly as the guard unlocked her cell. After bidding adieu to Dolly, she descended the same steps she had climbed eleven months earlier and left the cold prison a free woman. Like so many of her predecessors, she walked slowly south down the hill towards the main part of downtown Rawlins and slipped with scant notice into history.

SOURCES CITED

The primary source documents used in developing this story may be found in the Laramie County Third District Court Criminal Case File #4-220, *State of Wyoming v. Gerty Brown*; the Police Register for Cheyenne, Wyoming, 1906; the Justice of the Peace Dockets for A.E. Trump and W.P. Carroll; as well as the Wyoming State Penitentiary's inmate records for Gerty Brown, "Convict #1080."

Although there are few newspaper accounts about Gerty's activities, the articles "Gertie Brown May Face Burglary Charge," "Two Women Sentenced," and "Gertrude Up Against It," respectively, in the March 28, March 29, and April 2, 1907 *Cheyenne Daily Leader*, briefly describe Gerty's crime as well as the courtroom scene at the time of her sentencing.

Party Line Playmate

 NO ONE KNOWS WHAT hand he held. The queen of hearts, who stalked James E. Passwater, nearly trumped his life as he sat playing cards one evening at Smizer's Saloon in Encampment, Wyoming.

Passwater, a well-known *bon vivant* and the manager of the telephone system at the small copper mining boom town on the sunset side of the Snowy Range, apparently made his business doing pleasure with nineteen-year-old Anna Groves. And he did, if you believe Annie. She claimed Passwater infected her with "a bad dose of siphylis which was spread through her body until she [was] a mass of sores."

Despite her repeated notes pleading for him to call or to help pay her doctor bills, he refused. She alleged, too, that on at least one occasion, he beat her when she confronted him. Racked with pain and shame as her lower lip gave way to a huge, raw abscess, Annie became desperate and determined to kill the *roué*.

Her opportunity came the evening of October 15, 1907, as she saw him through a glass pane at the back of the saloon. Her onetime lover sat at a table, facing the window. Raising her pistol, she centered her sight on his head and pulled the trigger. Either her trembling rage forced the slug to stray or its impact against the glass changed its course, because the bullet missed its mark. But not by much. It passed through his hat brim and lodged in the shoulder of Louis Peterson, an innocent bystander.

Although details are sketchy, Passwater apparently fled to Justice of the Peace S.E. Ferree's office, where he filed a complaint that Annie:

> . . . did unlawfully, willfully and maliciously perpetrate an assault and battery upon him . . . with the intent to kill him, by shooting at him with a gun, a bullet from said gun grazing his . . . head.

Constable J.J. Wirth, who received the summons that night, quickly found and served Annie with the complaint before taking her into custody. Justice Ferree conducted the preliminary hearing that same evening. Upon being advised of her right to counsel and asking if she wished the complaint against her officially investigated, the young woman deferred for lack of funds. The court appointed an attorney named McMicken. After he heard her story, she followed his advice by throwing herself on the mercy of the court, hoping for the lightest sentence possible. She acknowledged being "guilty of the offense as charged."

Authorities immediately transferred her to the Carbon County Jail, where Sheriff E.M. Horton locked her away in a cell pending a hearing before the Third Judicial District Court already in session.

Only two days later, Carbon County Attorney and Prosecutor N.R. Greenfield filed his indictment against Annie charging that she:

> ... did then and there feloniously attempt to commit a violent injury in and upon the person of James Passwater, she the said Annie Groves, then and there having the present ability to commit said injury, by ... feloniously, purposely and with premeditated malice shooting at and upon the said ... Passwater with a certain loaded pistol ... held in the hands of said Annie Groves, with intent then and there and thereby him the said James Passwater, feloniously, purposely and with premeditated malice to kill and murder.

The court rendered its verdict nearly as quickly as the bullet did its damage to the bystander. Alone before the bench that Thursday, October 17, she heard the judge speak these words:

> It is therefore considered, ordered and adjudged by the Court, that you, Annie Groves, be taken by the Sheriff of Carbon County, State of Wyoming, and be by him delivered to the Warden or Keeper of said prison, and that you will there be imprisoned and confined according to the rules and regulations of said prison for the term of One (1) year at hard labor, and pay the costs of this action.

Annie Groves (Inmate #1148) missed when she fired a shot at the man who infected her with a virulent venereal disease that destroyed her lower lip. Regrettably, the bullet instead hit a bystander in the shoulder. Annie was sentenced to a year of "hard labor" in the Wyoming State Penitentiary. (Wyoming Division of Cultural Resources)

Sheriff Horton delivered her that same evening to the prison in Rawlins. There, during her in-processing, authorities learned that Annie, with her medium blond hair, had been born about 1888 in Kansas, where her parents raised her in the Methodist faith. They learned, too, that she received a ninth-grade education and, despite having worked as a prostitute, described her behavior as "temperate." Although her family still lived at that time, she refused to disclose their identity or whereabouts, listing only her husband, E.J. Groves, who remained in Encampment.

With his feminine nemesis securely tucked away in prison, Mr. Passwater "left for other parts." According to a local newspaper account, "the gentleman has a better job in a better place but are not prepared to say where."

Annie's spouse immediately went to work to secure a pardon from Governor Bryant B. Brooks. Only about two months after her incarceration, the first of three consecutive notices regarding his intent to seek her pardon appeared in the November 29 *Grand Encampment Herald*:

> Notice is hereby given that an application for pardon will be made to the State Board of Pardons by the undersigned on behalf of Anna Groves, who pleaded guilty by perpetrating a felonious assault upon J.E. Passwater at Encampment, Wyoming, October 15, 1907, and was sentenced by Hon. David H. Craig, Wyoming, October 17, 1907, to one year's imprisonment in the state penitentiary, said pardon to become effective after December 25, 1907. [signed] E.J. Groves

Following publication of those notices, Annie's deadbeat husband fled to his former home in Fremont, Nebraska, to avoid paying the newspaper for such announcements, a fact the *Herald* editor published for all to see.

Given the public sympathy generated by the perceived injustice in Annie's case, as well as her pitiful physical condition, the Board of Pardons responded to the petition, urging Governor Brooks on February 19, 1908, to grant a pardon. When he responded favorably the following March 2, Annie stepped from her third-floor cell, once again a free woman, having served less than five months of her one-year sentence. It is believed she rejoined her husband in Nebraska. So silently and swiftly did she leave prison that, upon learning of her release, the *Grand Encampment Herald* editor mused:

> . . . what has become of Mrs. Anna Groves, the woman sent from here for a year for shooting at J.E. Passwater the past summer. We hadn't heard of her pardon or escape and supposed she was still in the Rawlins pen.

SOURCES CITED

The Carbon County Criminal Case File #639, *State of Wyoming v. Anna Groves*; Justice of the Peace S.E. Ferree's Docket, and the Wyoming State Penitentiary's records regarding "Convict #1148," offer the most definitive information about Anna Groves and her imprisonment in the state pen.

Perhaps the most descriptive information available concerning her crime and subsequent trial can be found in the *Grand Encampment Herald* for the period of October 18, 1907, through June 6, 1908.

The Girl in the Freudian Slip

My little brother brought some caned plumbs from our ranch 1-1/2 mi from Smoot and we mixed it with more fruit. Mamma told me to make pies—My father had put poison in the can that came from the ranch with rat-poison—We didn't know it. Papa ate the pies first   in ten minutes he was in convulsions and was dead in fifteen minutes. I hope you will let me go home because I am guilty . . .
[signed] Miss Annie Bruce

Authorities claimed, following that slip of the lip, that Annie Florence Bruce told at least one other version about the death of her father. That first tale, in fact, left an aftertaste of doubt as bitter as the strychnine they believed she poured into the pie eaten by James Hamilton Bruce. As Uinta County

Attorney and Prosecutor D.G. Thomas recalled, he and Sheriff Jonathan Jones first questioned Annie about the crime in mid-June 1907. Although she admitted making the pie, she claimed to know nothing about the poison. She seemed so very nervous and agitated, however, that Thomas and Jones decided she must know more than she told them, so they arrested her and took her to the county jail, where she broke down and confessed the following:

> I, Annie Bruce, of Smoot, Uinta County, Wyoming, make the following statements of my own free will and accord, without any promise of reward from any one, and without compulsion or threats or hope of benefit to relieve my conscience of the guilt upon my soul.
>
> On the 20th day of March, A.D., 1907, I made five pies; while I was in the act of making the pies a feeling or a wish came over me to kill someone, and this feeling I could not resist. So I went to the store and procured a bottle of poison which I knew was there. I took the bottle of poison out of the lower box, which was full, and to do so I removed the upper box. When I secured the poison I put the upper box back on the lower box and went into the kitchen, and while no one was looking, I emptied the bottle of poison into the pie. The poison was strychnine. I put the poison into the last pie I made. In the morning ma and myself were preparing pa's lunch, and ma said to me, "Anna, fetch me a pie from the cupboard." I brought the pie which I had poisoned. I knew it was poisoned and this pie was afterwards sent by ma to the ranch. It was this pie that killed my pa. After pa died I felt awful sorry.

Anna Florence Bruce (Inmate #1206) confessed a crime so chilling, so compelling and unbelievable that it left the jury hearing her case with an aftertaste as bitter as the strychnine she poured into her father's plum pie. (Wyoming Division of Cultural Resources)

Bawled and cried a great deal. I yet feel awful sorry I put the poison in the pie that killed my pa.

I make this statement in the presence of D.G. Thomas . . . Jonathan Jones, Sheriff, and William DeLaney, Deputy Sheriff.

[signed] Annie Bruce.

Attorney Thomas said he wrote the substance of the statement, which the accused girl signed in his presence as well as that of the sheriff and the deputy.

But still other versions of the story surfaced. For example, Annie's namesake mother offered several accounts. She first suggested that, in making the fatal pie, perhaps she used an unwashed tin in which James previously had placed the poison. "Some farm animal had trampled on the pan," she said, "and filled it full of dents in which the strychnine might have lodged and thus been baked into the pie crust." Ten months later, she gave a different twist to the tale.

Mr. Bruce had been in the habit for a number of years of taking his lunch to the neighboring ranch where he and his boys were at work, and how, a few days before his death he took some dried fruit and poisoned it with strychnine for gophers, putting the fruit in a can and taking it with him to the ranch. Other business . . . took his attention, and the fruit was forgotten until one of the children sent to the ranch for some dishes returned home with a number of tins, including the bucket containing the fruit.

By an unfortunate coincidence Annie was just at that time making a batch of pies and, without knowing the fruit was poisoned, made a pie of it, which the next day [James] ate and immediately died.

Her son, James Laurence, however, added a most significant fact. While he and his father ate their pie in the field, the elder James almost immediately felt his stomach "attacked by intense pains." His father, the son said, "at once realized that he had been poisoned and told his son to preserve the remainder of the pie for use as evidence. Suspecting the pastry as the culprit, one of the Bruce boys fed a small portion to a nearby house cat that died swiftly. Bruce, too, succumbed within minutes. When Anna, young James's mother, arrived at her husband's body, she seized the incriminating pie and threw it into a creek before her son intervened.

Sadly, the victim never gave his account of the tragedy. It remains locked away forever in his grave. What is known is that the stern but respected forty-three-year-old Mormon died quickly and terribly.

Born on April 1, 1864, in Scotland, James Hamilton Bruce had emigrated at age six to the United States with his parents. Although little is known about his early manhood, he married Anna Elizabeth Clark in Logan, Utah, on October 9, 1885. They subsequently moved east to Almy, a small coal mining community in southwestern Wyoming, where she gave birth to their first child, James Laurence. A daughter, Jeannet, came the following spring only to die four and a half months later. Mrs. Bruce immediately became pregnant with her third, and namesake, child, Anna Florence. Then, sometime between Annie's birth on June 25, 1889, and that of her younger brother, Robert

Hamilton, in February 1891, Mr. Bruce moved his growing family to Cottonwood, renamed Smoot later that same year. There the couple quickly added four more children— Joseph Wallace (October 1892), Stella ("Stellie," December 1894), Glennis (October 1896), and Ella Vietta ("Ellie," May 1899)—before James left his family to go on a two-year Mormon church mission to Michigan. During that trip, however, major signs of trouble surfaced for the Bruce family. Despite James's extended absence, his thirty-two-year-old spouse found herself pregnant. As tongues wagged and the local brethren counted suspiciously upon their fingers, another Bruce child arrived approximately eleven months after James's departure.

Despite Anna's suspected peccadillo, James returned home and resumed a relationship with his wife. His brood continued to expand with Speers (perhaps Spiers, born 1901), Elizabeth (born 1902 or 1903), Ernest Leroy (May 1904), and Isabella (July 1905).

The dour, thrifty Scotsman also established a small store in Smoot and bought some land, which he ranched on the outskirts of the town. Annie's attorney, J.H. Ryckman, offered his own variation about circumstances that led to James's death. Mr. Bruce, like other settlers, Ryckman said, poisoned mountain rats and other varmints that preyed upon their crops. In fact, five days before James's death, the lawyer continued, the elder Bruce:

> ... asked his daughter, Annie, for cheese which he intended to poison with strychnine and take down to the little cabin on the ranch where the rats were annoying.

Upon being told that there was no cheese he asked impatiently, "Well, what have you got?" She answered, "nothing but dried fruit." He said, "give me that" and on receiving the fruit which was in a molasses can [he] proceeded to sprinkle a half bottle of strychnine into it and take it down to the ranch with him.

There it remained until the morning . . . when Mrs. Bruce and Annie needed some pie tins and sent one of the children down to the ranch to bring back a number of pans which his father had allowed to accumulate at the cabin after the fashion of men. The boy gathered up all the tin ware he could find and brought back the can of poisoned plums as well as the pans. Mrs. Bruce and Annie prepared and baked four pies but found they did not have enough fruit for a fifth.

As Mrs. Bruce was handling the tins she found that one of the cans was half full of dried plums and used them to complete the filling of the fifth pie. She then put the five pies away on a shelf until the next day when she cut three of them to put into the lunches which were sent to the ranch and to the school which part of her children attended. Her favorite son, [Joseph] Wallace, accompanied his father to the ranch on the day of the alleged murder and thus ran the risk of eating a part of the poisoned pie. It so happened, however, that the father ate his share first and the boy was saved from death.

George W. Bruce, a brother of the deceased James, disputed Ryckman's account, testifying that at least one of his nephews told him that James Hamilton Bruce "never used poison to kill rats, mice or other animals." Ryckman countered, however, that he did not believe Annie capable of deliberately killing her dad. She, he said, "was her father's favorite child and was as fond of him as he was of her." Annie's brothers and sisters vouched for Ryckman's assessment and agreed "the father and eldest daughter were on the best of terms." Their relationship notwithstanding, the elder James breathed no more and someone had caused his death.

Two days after the tragedy, Justice of the Peace W.R. Tolman, from Fairview, a small neighboring town to the northwest, held an inquest at James's home. As acting coroner, he subpoenaed numerous witnesses, including several of Annie's siblings, for the one P.M. event, where they gave testimony before a jury consisting of O.T. Papworth, Wilford W. Cranney, and W.J. Jensen. After the jurors satisfied themselves as to the facts, their foreman, Papworth, announced, to no one's surprise, "That James Bruce came to his death by eating pie which contained poison which was in the pie before he took it from his home in Smoot Wyo. on the morning of the 21st of March A.D. 1907, and that he died at his ranch one and one quarter miles from his home . . . about 10:30 A.M. of said date."

After carefully removing and preserving James's stomach and liver, Justice Tohman sent the organs to Professor Henry G. Knight, the state chemist, for analysis. Knight concluded that of the three mouthfuls of pie eaten by James, part went into his liver and was absorbed. His stomach tissue absorbed another segment of the dessert. The amount of strychnine that remained in the stomach, however, "was sufficient to have killed five men," said Knight.

Shortly after that diagnosis, the *Afton Independent* published a notice from George Bruce, brother of James, exonerating Anna Bruce and her family from all blame. He later retracted that statement, claiming he only inserted the notice in the paper "because Mrs. Bruce and Annie had begged him to." In the meantime, Sheriff Jones and County Attorney Thomas went to Smoot, where they spent several days in June investigating the case.

Despite a sizeable body of evidence indicating foul play, Attorney Thomas still waited roughly four and a half months before he directed Sheriff Jones to serve separate bench warrants to apprehend Mrs. Bruce and her seventeen-year-old daughter Annie. In reporting their arrest, newspapers described the pair as "refined in appearance, have quiet voices, and a pleasant manner. They are both of medium height, are both slender and have remarkably bright, brown eyes and hair of a much lighter shade." Reporters also described the English-born Mrs. Bruce as a "pretty woman." Following their apprehension at their home in Smoot on August 8, the seemingly unconcerned women returned with the lawman to Evanston, where he imprisoned them in the Uinta County Jail until the District Court of the Third Judicial District convened that September. Professor Knight, one of the prosecution's most important witnesses, became ill, however, so the presiding judge postponed the case until the following April. In the meantime, Mrs. Bruce and Annie each raised ten thousand dollars bail—thanks to Mrs. Bruce's father, James Farnsworth Clark, and friends Joseph and Jack Reeves of Afton—and so gained temporary freedom on September 5.

Prior to leaving the jail, where they met with their bene-factors and attorney Ryckman, Annie and her mother thanked Deputy Sheriff William C. Deloney for his kind-nesses during their incarceration. Looking forward to returning home, Mrs. Bruce spoke tenderly of rejoining her ten children. Annie, too, "was trembling with eagerness to return to her free life at the ranch." She said, "The first thing I am going to do is get on my old pet [horse] and go after the cows." The pair also spoke of their coming trial with "apparent stoicism and cheerfulness, asserting their innocence and their belief that they would be acquitted."

Some seven months later, the District Court was recon-vened by Judge David H. Craig on April 10, 1908, in Evanston. Long before the appointed hour arrived, anxious spectators packed the courtroom to hear the lurid evidence of James's poisoning. Attorney M.C. Brown, of Laramie, assisted Thomas in prosecuting the case while John A. Bagley, a former Attorney General of the State of Idaho, aided Ryckman's defense of the women. Although apparently alert to every word, spectators said Annie appeared "quite indifferent" to the proceedings. Her mother, however, "was extremely nervous and followed every word spoken by the court lawyers and witnesses."

When the defense attorneys presented evidence that the strychnine came from James's store in Smoot, the prosecutor countered with some new evidence of his own. On the con-trary, the defense attorney claimed, the murderer had retrieved the poison from a high shelf in James's ranch shed. And in doing so, he said, climbed up to reach for it and left a palm print in dust there. "As Mr. Bruce had a large hand," added Thomas, "it was not he who got it, and the state will try to prove that Miss Bruce is the one who got it as her hand exactly fits the imprint."

The defense team severely cross-examined Deputy Deloney, who claimed that he witnessed Annie's confession and the subsequent signing of her transcribed statement. The defense contended that Annie signed her name to a blank piece of paper that the prosecution later filled with statements pertaining to the crime. When Deloney refused to refute his earlier testimony, Defense Attorney Ryckman tried to prove that he, the sheriff, and the prosecutor "bull-dozed" Annie into signing the empty form.

The following day Annie took the stand. For three hours, she resisted every attempt by the prosecutors to wring an admission of guilt from her. "They are liars," she said, "when they [the deputy, sheriff, and prosecutor] say I signed that paper after it was written!" In fact, she branded all of the prosecution's witnesses as "liars."

After two days of testimony and the cross-examination of twenty witnesses for the prosecution and twelve for the defense, all parties completed their arguments at 9:15 P.M. on April 13. Faced with their awesome task, the jurors left the court to decide whether 1) Annie had murdered her father or 2) the prosecution's witnesses had lied under oath and fabricated evidence.

Following lengthy deliberations that evening, jury foreman Al Osterhout polled his fellow jurors. That first count of ballots showed a split decision, with seven voting to acquit while five favored a "manslaughter" verdict. Throughout the night, the jury continued to argue the evidence. Not until three o'clock that afternoon (April 14) did bailiff Samuel Blackham quietly approach the bench to announce a decision. Soon thereafter the judge ordered the jury members to return to the courtroom. After they took their seats, Clerk of Court John S. Johnston accepted their written decision, then handed it to the judge. As those who packed the courtroom looked on, the foreman announced that the jury found Annie "guilty of manslaughter." As the word "guilty" fell from the clerk's lips, a deafening clap of thunder shook the walls while rain and hail pelted the windows of the courthouse.

In a postscript to the verdict, jury foreman Osterhout said, "The jury in the above case, request the leniency of the Court." Hearing those words, Annie simply sighed an audible "Oh!" She buried her face against her mother's breast before they fell into each other's arms and "wept in deep anguish." That scene of sadness continued until Sheriff Jones led Annie, supported by the arm of her mother, away to her cell. With Annie's conviction, prosecutor Thomas immediately dropped his case against her mother citing a lack of evidence.

Unknown to the principals, the same evening the jurors considered their verdict, Annie's supporters busily circulated petitions for her pardon. Strangely, some of the names of the same jurors who found her guilty appeared among the more than 630 signers.

Less than a week later, Judge Craig brought Annie back before his bench, where he pronounced his sentence: " ... four years in the penitentiary at Rawlins." The following day, Sheriff Jones loaded Annie and seven male prisoners aboard a train and escorted the group east to Rawlins, where

authorities imprisoned them in the Wyoming State Penitentiary. As the only woman inmate there at the time, the
guards kept Annie "apart from the other convicts and put
[her] to mending, washing and similar work to which she is
accustomed." Prosecutor Thomas said later that while en
route to prison, Annie admitted to the sheriff and one of the
guards "that when she denied it [the crime] she told a lie,
and that the signed statement was the truth, that she had
been advised to tell a lie on the witness stand."

Several weeks later, Mrs. Bruce and her father traveled
to Cheyenne and they met with Governor Joseph M. Carey
to seek his pardon for Annie. On their way back westward,
they stopped at the prison in Rawlins, where they met with
Annie. They found her "being well treated . . . but is ever
hopeful that either a pardon or some new evidence may
appear to bring her release."

In the meantime, the notorious bootlegger and horse
thief Ella "Bronco Nell" Smith joined Annie in the women's
ward. In fact, some suggest that Annie's exposure to such
disreputable company encouraged her family to push,
through their attorney, to get Annie either pardoned or
moved to what they considered a more favorable environment at the state prison in Cañon City, Colorado. Two
months later (mid-July 1908), Mrs. Bruce and her father
returned to Cheyenne for another meeting with the governor, but again they failed to gain Annie's early release or her
transfer to another penal facility.

Not until October 7, 1909, did the Bruce family, with
the aid of their state senator, Wilford A. Hyde, finally get
Annie transferred to the Colorado State Penitentiary. During

her subsequent imprisonment there, her family and friends continued to seek her release. As late as March 15, 1911, in fact, nearly one hundred individuals signed a petition requesting Governor Carey's intervention and support. Toward that end, Mrs. Bruce added her own plaintive plea (printed here as written):

> I wrote you in behalf of my daughter Miss Annie Bruce who is serving a sentence in Canon City, Colo. Who was deeply wronged of he papa death and humble ask you Govornor to Pardon my innocent child she almost heart broken to get home to her Mamma I sincerely ask you Governor with all my heart for the freedom of my child   praying you will sympathize with me is my humble prayer
>
>   [signed] Mrs. Annie E. Bruce

Her plea fell on deaf ears, however, as the Board of Pardons denied the appeal when the group met several weeks later. That refusal probably didn't surprise either Annie or her mother, because they must have known that some very influential Smoot neighbors opposed the pardon. In a letter written to Governor Carey's predecessor, Governor B.B. Brooks, they revealed some previously undiscussed information.

> Your Honor, I hold the office of presiding Bishop here and live within one hundred yards of the family, was with Mr Bruce when he died, have been a witness in court in fact have thoroughly investigated the case and am sure that she has had a fair and impartial trial and given a light sentence for so serious a crime and there is no question of her guilt. We are

also of the opinion that the mother is also implicated in the crime and that confinement in prison will cause the young woman to divulge the secrets of the atrocious crime

Threats are being made by the mother and her family as to what will happen when Annie is pardoned

I am sure your Honor has followed this case and have no need of being given any information regarding it   We have no particular fault to find with the outcome of this trial but for reasons which are sure to appeal to you we do not wish the judgment of the court set aside   It may seem unsympathetic to take the matter up in this way but sometimes sympathy over releases justice. Now we as neighbors are well acquainted with the families of Mr. and Mrs. Bruce.

Mr. Bruce was an honorable, honest, God fearing, worthy citizen, true to his convictions, but unhappily married to a woman of vicious habits, bad tempered, revengeful who to spite her husband once set fire to their own barn, and while her husband was away doing missionary work she mingled with more of her kind and Eleven months after he went away became the mother of a child which of course was not his.

This could only result in heartache and pain to the husband making his relations with her strained and unhappy but he made the best of it and went to work from which he never seemed to tire   His Brother and sisters are good honest citizens and the right kind of people to make a porpurious law-abiding community while her family are not of good morals and as the

Honorable judge said is giving his charge to the jury they are "degerates."

[signed] Bishop Frank P. Cranney, Chas. H. Peterson (school trustee), Chas. A. Johnson (school trustee), Wilber T. Cranney (Sunday school supt.), R.P. Baldwin (principal of day school), Thomas Walton (justice of Peace), G.W. Bruce (brother of deceased) and Mrs. C.H. Peterson (sister of deceased)

But in the end, this same evidence also, perhaps, encouraged Governor Carey's compassion, for he finally pardoned Annie in June 1911. In support of that decision, he claimed the State Board of Pardons recommended that action despite the fact that only two months earlier (April 5) the same Board met and specifically refused to consider Annie's case. Nevertheless, Annie gained freedom from the Colorado State Penitentiary on June 6, 1911 . . . only eight days before her earliest possible discharge date.

Whether motivated by politics, compassion, or simply because of the Mormon leaders' suggestion that Annie's mother used her as an unwilling accomplice, the governor's action freed the girl to start a new life. After later moving to Idaho Falls, Idaho, Annie married Arthur S. Smith, a miner, on July 5, 1913. They subsequently went on to Eureka, Utah, where Arthur's "Aunty Nellie Smith" resided. There she gave birth to two sons and a daughter. Annie remained in Eureka trying to resurrect her reputation until her life ended at age eighty-six, after a long illness, on August 13, 1975, in the nearby Payson, Utah, hospital.

Sources Cited

Much can be learned about Annie Bruce's story through the study of Uinta County District Court Criminal Case Files #97 and #98—*State of Wyoming v. Annie Bruce*—as well as Uinta County Inquest Case File #70. For physical details regarding the woman, I know of nothing as informative as the Wyoming and Colorado State Penitentiary files, respectively, regarding "Convict #1206" and "Convict #7572." But of all such information, nothing proved quite so helpful as that information provided by Bruce family members interested in better understanding their relatives' histories.

Detailed information regarding the Bruce family's history is contained in the LDS microfiche records on file at the Laramie County Library as well as in the 1900 U.S. Census records for Michigan (regarding James Bruce's church mission) and for Wyoming.

Petitions for Pardon Files and the correspondence and letterbooks of Governors Carey and Brooks also provide a wealth of previously unpublished details concerning background about the Bruces as well as machinations by that family and its attorney on behalf of Annie's pardon.

And the following newspapers, of course, offer voluminous information, not only concerning the crime, but details pertaining to Annie's criminal trial: Afton's *Star Valley Independent*, Evanston's *Wyoming Press*, and the *Cheyenne Daily Leader* (March 1907 through April 1908).

Definitive information concerning Annie's life and death in Eureka, Utah, is published in the *Eureka Reporter's* August 22, 1975, obituary headlined "Annie B. Smith, local resident, passes away."

Branded

FLANKED BY A mass of floral offerings and faced by many mourners, Reverend R.N. Buswell undoubtedly sensed the high esteem in which many people of Meeteetse, Wyoming, held the lady in the casket that Friday, February 1, 1952. The solemnity of his Presbyterian service and the frocked trio, who sang "In the Garden" and "God Will Take Care of You," did not seem to dampen the sense that this was no ordinary funeral . . . no ordinary woman.

The minister's eulogy stated that Mrs. Ella Craig, whose health declined during the previous six months, had died at her nearby ranch home, where she had lived for more than forty years. Then, following a benediction prayer, her husband George Craig, a son, and a daughter interred her in the Meeteetse Cemetery.

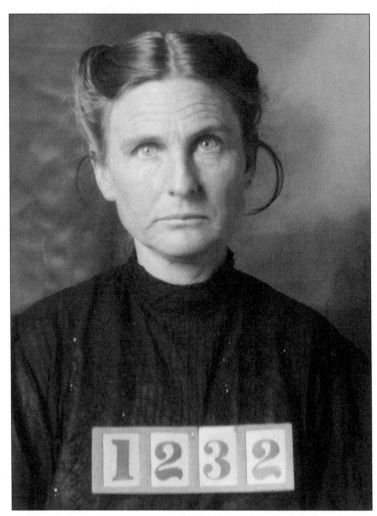

Ella "Bronco Nell" Smith (Inmate #1232) supported herself as a freighter and bootlegger until 1907 when authorities arrested and convicted her for feloniously putting her brand on two of her neighbor's colts. (Wyoming Division of Cultural Resources)

Most of those who attended the services paid homage to their neighbor and honored her contributions as a local pioneer. A few of her peers, however, may have stifled whispered asides, because they remembered the deceased not as the venerable Mrs. Ella Craig but as Mrs. Ella "Bronco Nell" Smith, a convicted bootlegger and horse thief, who held the ignominious distinction of being the last woman to serve time in the Wyoming State Penitentiary at Rawlins.

THE TRAIL DRIVE NORTH

Although nothing seems to be documented about "Mrs. Smith," or how Ella spent the first three decades of her life, the lady with the light blue eyes and dark gray-streaked hair claimed that she and her daughter, Ruth, drove their seven mustangs north from Texas and into Wyoming around the turn of the century. At the end of that dusty journey, they settled in Meeteetse, a town whose name comes from the Shoshone Indian word for "meeting place" or "place of rest." The sleepy town, with its false-fronted and pressed-brick buildings linked loosely by warped boardwalks, rests on the southeast bank of the upper Greybull River. That river, in turn, drains the eastern slopes of the Absaroka Mountains. There the trim woman, with a fifth-grade education, struggled to feed herself and her child by raising horses and doing some freighting. Although she claimed to follow the Seventh Day Adventist faith, her belief proved weak in that she occasionally supplemented their meager income by illegally making and selling liquor. That practice, however, came to a screeching halt on November 12, 1905, when she pled "guilty" to the federal offense of selling a quart of booze to two local Crow Indians named Ben Hillside and James Carpenter. Not until the following April 5, however, did Judge John A. Riner of the Fourth Judicial District Court in Cheyenne pronounce judgment by fining her one hundred dollars plus court costs and ordering U.S. Marshal L.G. Davis to lock her away for sixty days in the Laramie County jail. Embarrassing? Probably. The end of her problems with the law? Definitely not!

It fact, only about five and a half months later (November 18, 1907), Ella again found herself before the bench. This time, Big Horn County Deputy Sheriffs Hubbard and Pierce arrested Ella and her part-time hired hand, Joseph B. Shupp, for suspected rustling. Five days later, the authorities moved the couple to Basin, Wyoming, where Justice of the Peace O.J. Robertson charged them with "unlawfully and feloniously" stealing from neighboring rancher John Milton Baldwin two colts valued at thirty-five dollars each. After pronouncing that official complaint, he bound them over to the Fourth Judicial District Court. Their stay in jail, however, was brief thanks to the financial help of a friend, J.D. Bramnum. After providing a $1,500 surety bond for Ella, he also helped Ella post Shupp's bail.

Ella's respite from legal problems proved short-lived. On April 18, 1908, Big Horn County and Prosecuting Attorney C.A. Zaring exacerbated the defendants' problems by filing a district court indictment charging that Ella and Shupp "on or about 1st day of October A.D. 1907 . . . did then and there unlawfully feloniously brand two horses . . . with intent then and thereby to steal said animals." Although the court decided to try Ella and Shupp separately, the prosecutor later dropped the charges against Shupp for lack of evidence. That decision, however, did not deter Zaring's interest in seeking Ella's conviction.

COLT CASE GOES TO COURT

In the court case that followed at nine A.M. on Saturday, May 2, Baldwin testified that two of his mares, bearing his unique "dumbbell" brand, foaled in the spring of 1907. He remembered distinctly, he said, that he turned the pairs out on the range when the foals reached one or two months old. Baldwin recalled, too, that the colts' coats mirrored the colors of their respective mothers: a bay and a sorrel. He next saw the mares and their unbranded offspring together about October 9 that same year, he said. Another witness for the prosecution claimed that three days later he, too, saw the mares, but without their suckling colts.

Baldwin's neighbor O.B. Mann also remembered seeing the horses about the same time running up and down the fence line, trying to get out. He added,

> We examined the brands. The bay mare . . . had a "dumbbell" on her right shoulder . . . The dumbbell . . . was very dim. She had to be standing right or with the sun on it to see it at all, although it showed the full brand. [The dumbbell on the sorrel mare] was very plain only the bottom. It did not show the bottom of the lower circle.

Continuing, Mann said that, after bringing the mares back down to his place, "I decided to put them in the lower pasture next to the river, and notify Mr. Baldwin I had them there." He also claimed, "I got the colts the next day after the mares were supposed to be taken the night before." The colts, he added, closely resembled the mares: "A sorrel and a bay, I would think five-and-a-half to six months old." The difference, however, was that the colts sported Ella's "N bar triangle" brand on their left shoulders, "very plain and very fresh . . . still black from branding." They remained there about a week, he said, before he noticed that "My fence was torn down and they. . . had left the pasture." He remembered, too, that he saw Ella the previous evening, dressed in her usual garb of men's clothes and black work hat, riding on the neighboring lease. "She came along where we were working on a ridge with a bunch of horses . . . . She passed where we were working."

During subsequent cross-examination, Baldwin told Zaring that he next saw the stock in question about October 25 on Whitney's lease. After removing them, he drove them down to O.P. Mann's place, where he put the two mares and the two colts into the corral. "The sorrel mare's colt went to sucking right immediately; the bay mare fought the colt for a while but finally it sucked," he said. Like the colts Mann described, both had "an N Triangle brand on the left shoulder." The stock, according to Mann, came from a piece of property he let Ella use "right across where the mares were in." The property along Iron Creek was about a quarter of a mile above Mann's ranch and about two and a half miles from Meeteetse, where Ella kept about forty head of range horses. "She asked permission to use it for a few saddle horses," Mann said; "I said I would not hire it to her, but would not object if she kept horses there a few days."

About three weeks after taking the stock back to his place, and with the evidence of Ella's brand on his colt, Baldwin filed a complaint with local authorities, who issued a warrant for her arrest. Upon learning of the rancher's allegations, forty-year-old ranch hand Chris Teeter, who worked occasionally for Baldwin, went to his friend Ella and warned her. Ella immediately called upon Baldwin to try to resolve the matter. Baldwin recalled her visit:

> She told me when she came up that she understood I had a couple of colts with her brand on, I told her there was and I pointed them out to her. She asked if she could not swap a couple of colts or buy them. I told her, no, I didn't want to sell them at all. Then she wanted to know if there was any way she could settle it. I said, I guess not, it was gone to far now. She said it would not look so bad if she was not a lone woman and I ought not to be hard on with her. I told her if she was a lone woman it would be different, but she had _____ hanging around there stealing horses.

Never did he give her permission, he said, to brand his horses. When Baldwin refused to negotiate or settle, Ella rushed next to see attorney H.S. Ridgley of the firm Ridgley and West.

THE LONG SHADOW OF THE WYOMING STOCK GROWERS ASSOCIATION

But there seemed to be more to Baldwin's story than he seemed willing to recall. During the defense attorney's cross-examination in court, Ridgley asked:

Q: Isn't it true in addition to telling her it had gone too far, you also told her the stockmen [Wyoming Stock Growers Association] wouldn't let you dismiss the case?

A: I don't remember whether I told her that or not. I did tell her I could not drop it if I wanted to.

Q: Didn't you tell her the stockmen would not let you drop it?

A: I cannot tell that.

Q: Didn't you tell her you yourself would be willing to fix up the matter, but the stockmen would not?

A: I didn't tell her that.

Q: But you did tell her the stockmen would not let you do it?

A: I might have said something about the Association. I don't remember mentioning stockmen.

Without being more specific, Baldwin's disclosure about the role of the Stock Growers Association landed like a small bomb in the midst of the testimony. It also gave credence to the long-held rumor that members of the cowmen's cabal did not abide what its members perceived as uppity women playing fast and loose with rules their male counterparts held so dear. Another Ella—"Cattle Kate" Watson—learned that lesson the hard way nearly eighteen years earlier (June 20, 1889), when a band of cattle barons gave that woman and her common-law husband, James Averell, a long swing on a pair of short ropes in the shadow of Independence Rock.

ELLA TELLS HER STORY

In Ridgley's direct examination of Ella, she readily acknowledged that she branded Baldwin's colts: "I guess I did . . . I took them [eight head of horses] including the . . . colts, but not following any mares off the range near Iron Creek . . . . One was a bay colt. I don't know whether you would call it a bay or not, between a bay and a brown; the other was a sorrel colt." The four-to-five-month-old colts, she added, matched the color of several mares that she ran on her own range.

She brought them into Meeteetse, she said, via a main road and past a "Mr. Gould's" place en route to her spread east of town. Her large corral fronted Main Street. There, in her barn on the northeast side of the river, she claimed that on September 27 or 28—about a week earlier than the dates alleged by Baldwin and Mann—she threw and branded the two colts by herself. After marking the stock, she said she kept them corralled until the next evening, then turned them out to pasture. "Drove them through town—They went past Goulds—out in the hills . . . off on the open range southwest of town . . . I never saw the colts after I branded then," she concluded.

After listening to the closing testimony on May 20, it took the all-male jury only a couple of hours before arriving at a verdict. Announcing the jurors' decision, their foreman Dan Crain stated, "We the jury, duly sworn and empanelled in the above entitled action, do find the defendant Ella Smith, guilty as charged in the Information and do find the value of the property branded, to be $50.00."

Exactly one week later, Judge Parmalee recalled Ella from her cell at the courthouse and sentenced her to eighteen months in Wyoming's state penitentiary. Ridgley immediately filed a motion for a new trial on the basis of his belief that the evidence, as presented, failed to sustain the jury's verdict. On June 13, however, the court instructed the Big Horn County sheriff to take Ella into his custody and deliver her to the prison in Rawlins. There she remained until, after serving eighteen months and earning two months' "good time," Warden G.D. Lewis discharged her on September 16, 1909, "by reason of Expiration of sentence."

Soon thereafter, she returned to her ranch near Meeteetse, where she quietly and unobtrusively resumed life with her daughter. They remained there until she met a reputed drunk and rounder named George Craig, whose nefarious reputation nearly matched her own, and they married at seven P.M. on July 25, 1939, in a civil ceremony at Thermopolis, Wyoming.

Who knows for whom this lass waits, at the north side of the Wyoming State Penitentiary at Rawlins. Some may think she pines for her father, brother, or lover. Or does she yearn instead for the return of her mother or sister, paying dearly for her sins against society. (Wyoming Frontier Prison and Carbon County Museum)

SOURCES CITED

The primary documents used in developing this story
may be found in the Big Horn County District Criminal
Case File #358; Justice Docket, Big Horn County, Vol. I
(February, 1906-January, 1911); Sheriff's Register of Pris-
oners, Big Horn County; Wyoming State Penitentiary
Inmate File #1232, and *Wyoming Reports*, Cases Decided in
the Supreme Court of Wyoming from May 12, 1908, to
June 2, 1909, reported by Charles N. Potter, Vol. 17
(Laramie, Wyoming: The Laramie Republic Co., 1909).
The aforementioned records can be found at the Wyoming
State Archives. Another major primary source researched
for this story was the U.S.A. *District of Wyoming v. Ella
Smith*, District Court, Eighth Judicial District of Wyoming, Criminal Case Files, 1890-1925, Box #12, which is
on file at the National Archives, Rocky Mountain Region,
in Denver, Colorado.

Additional sources which proved very helpful in understanding Ella Smith's story included articles in the *Cody
Enterprise* ("Mrs. George Craig is Buried Friday," February
7, 1952, p. 6), the *Annals of Wyoming* ("Freight and Stage
Road from Rawlins to Red Lodge, Montana," Vol. 49, No.
2, pp. 265-266), and the Hot Springs County Clerk Marriage Records (Vol. #4, p. 296).

Epilogue

BUT THE PETTICOAT prisoners' stories did not end with the pardon and release of Annie Bruce. As early as mid-January 1909, the Wyoming State Board of Charities and Reform (SBCR) recognized Wyoming lacked sufficient women prisoners to warrant the employment of a full-time matron to look after such felons imprisoned at the penitentiary in Rawlins. Therefore, the SBCR enlisted the support of Governor Bryant B. Brooks, who, in his address to the Tenth State Legislature that year, recommended "our laws be so amended as to permit the sentencing of female prisoners to penal institutions of other states."

The Legislature responded by giving the governor authority to commute the sentences of such prisoners already convicted and serving time in the state penitentiary at Rawlins. Further, the Legislature authorized the SBCR's secretary "to communicate with the authorities of Colorado and Nebraska asking for rules and regulations and conditions under which female convicts . . . may be received from the State." And it recommended that those persons whose sentences were commuted be transferred to like institutions in other states with which the SBCR might make contracts for such confinement.

During subsequent communications, the SBCR determined Nebraska's daily fee of $1.50 per prisoner was exorbitant, but the following February, Colorado's Governor John F. Shafroth reported that "there was sufficient room in the Penitentiary in the female ward to accommodate from fifteen to twenty females in the new building just constructed." He said, too, that Colorado would accept female convicts from Wyoming at a price of one dollar per day. The SBCR, however, which regarded even this amount as too expensive, instructed its clerk to contact Utah and Idaho to ascertain under what terms those authorities might accept Wyoming's women prisoners.

For whatever reasons, the SBCR apparently eliminated those latter states from consideration and, at its June 7, 1909, meeting in Lander, authorized its clerk to accept the contract previously offered by Colorado Governor John F. Shafroth. When the SBCR's members reconvened the following month (July 14), they directed their clerk to return the signed contract to the proper Colorado authorities for final approval and implementation. Not until October 6 of that year did the state send Annie Bruce south to Cañon City, Colorado, where she became Wyoming's first woman in the Colorado State Penitentiary as its Inmate #7572.

CAÑON CITY, COLORADO

Although things went relatively well with that arrangement, it came undone nearly twenty-one years and twenty-two prisoners later when a female inmate prisoner at the Cañon City facility threatened the life of Geneva Collett, a Sheridan woman serving a life sentence for first-degree murder. According to correspondence from the Colorado State Penitentiary's Warden F.E. Crawford:

> ... a colored girl attacked a matron with a pair of scissors last December [1928]. Geneva intercepted and saved the life of the matron, thereby incurring the hatred of the colored girl. Warden Crawford has this girl locked up but he is thinking of releasing her in a week or ten days and does not want to be responsible for what might happens when she is released.

Although reasons for the Wyoming SBCR's actions are not clear, its officers instructed its secretary during its February 3, 1930, meeting "to advise Warden Crawford that the SBCR will try to make other arrangements for the Wyoming women prisoners but in the meantime urge that every precaution be taken to safeguard them at Cañon City."

Wyoming's State Auditor Roscoe Alcorn, also a member of the SBCR, reported that he and members of his facility search committee planned to visit the Nebraska, Kansas, and Oklahoma State Penitentiaries later that month to ask if any of those prisons might take women from Wyoming.

LANSING, KANSAS

The SBCR's secretary reported at the March 10 meeting that she received nine unfavorable replies to her letters to twelve states regarding custody of women prisoners. "The State of Nebraska," however, she said, "offers to take care of our prisoners at the rate of one dollar and sixty two cents per day which is their per capita cost." Mr. Alcorn added that during his trip, the Kansas institution for women very much impressed him and members of his committee. Continuing he said:

> They use a cottage system and for two years there had not been an escape. They now have 475 prisoners. They keep them employed at housework and farm work. They have an orchard in connection with the farm and they carry on some special industries such as basket-making. The work seemed to be organized very efficiently.

When Alcorn advised Mrs. Julia Perry, superintendent of the Kansas State Industrial Farm for Women, that the SBCR wished "to make arrangements for boarding women prisoners at a cost of not more than $1.25 per day," she promised to recommend that Governor C.M. Reed of Kansas approve that proposal. Before the following April 7 meeting, Wyoming's Governor and President of the SBCR Frank C. Emerson received this March 28 message from his Kansas counterpart:

> ORDERED, by the State board of Administration, that the Women's Industrial Farm in Lansing [Kansas] shall receive the women prisoners from the State of Wyoming,

give them the same care and treatment as those committed from Kansas, and use reasonable diligence to keep
them in custody. This shall be the extent of responsibility
of the institution and the Board of Administration. In
return the State of Wyoming shall pay to the Superintendent of the Women's Industrial Farm $1.50 per day for
the care of each prisoner, remittance to be made quarterly.

Upon the endorsement of Governor Emerson, the
SBCR accepted the Kansas offer and directed A.S. Roach,
Warden of the Colorado State Penitentiary, and his Super-
vising Matron, Miss Amy G. Abbott, to begin the transfer
of Wyoming women prisoners, effective May 1, 1930, from
their institution to the Women's Industrial Farm in Lansing.

Apparently that arrangement worked quite well at first,
because the Wyoming's SBCR reported in 1934:

Arrangements made with the State Industrial Farm for
Women at Lansing, Kansas, have proven so satisfactory
that they have been continued.... The women are
given excellent training, careful supervision, and
understanding treatment by the officials in charge;
with a reasonable fee of $1.50 per day for this care.

During the period of this report [1932-1934] but
one woman has been sentenced to a penitentiary term
and six others have been cared for at the Industrial
Farm. The cost of care and transportation amounted
to $5,656.06.

BACK TO COLORADO

Roughly two years later (March 2, 1936), after seventeen more Wyoming inmates served time in the Kansas

facility, history repeated itself. Colorado State Penitentiary Warden Roy Best contacted Wyoming's SBCR and advised that his institution "is now equipped with a new building for women prisoners" and he offered to care for Wyoming's female inmates at a bargain one dollar per day. Pleased with the possibility of saving fifty cents a day per prisoner compared to the rate in Kansas, Wyoming's SBCR, led by Governor Leslie A. Miller, immediately recommended—and its members carried the motion—that the secretary confer with Warden Alex McPherson. If the arrangement seemed feasible and the warden agreed, the SBCR ordered that arrangements should be made for the transfer of Wyoming's women from Kansas back to Colorado at the earliest possible date.

Again, for almost two decades, all went relatively well for about thirty-one Wyoming inmates in the care of Cañon City authorities until January 4, 1954, when Governor C.J. "Doc" Rogers told the SBCR he had received a letter from Colorado State Penitentiary Warden Harry Tinsley, "advising that the women's quarters are filled to capacity and that the State of Colorado cannot accept any more Wyoming Female Prisoners until such time as a vacancy occurs."

Anticipating such action, the SBCR secretary advised that he already had sent letters to Montana, Utah, Idaho, Michigan, and Nebraska to determine whether any of those states might consider accepting Wyoming women inmates on a contract basis.

YORK, NEBRASKA

At the SBCR's February 1, 1954, meeting, Governor Rogers told the members that although he had received replies from the various states, "Nebraska was the only state that has the space to care for the Female Prisoners." Following a formal inspection the following month of Nebraska's facility by Secretary E.C. Rothwell and several other SBCR members, their entire group reconvened March 8 to consider its options. According to minutes of the meeting, Miss Edna B. Stolt, State Superintendent of Public Education, "moved that the proposed contract with the State of Nebraska at the rate of $3.00 per day per prisoner be approved." Others seconded and carried the motion before Governor Rogers signed the contract and instructed Wyoming State Penitentiary Warden Dean Miller "to deliver any female prisoners sentenced from the State of Wyoming to the Reformatory for Women, State of Nebraska, York, Nebraska, in accordance with the contract."

More than two decades passed before the problem of incarcerating Wyoming's women prisoners resurfaced. At the June 23, 1976, meeting of the Wyoming SBCR, its members learned that "Housing women at York is very tenuous at the present time with possible rejections by July of '77." The SBCR members recognized that once more they must deal with the issue of housing and caring for its own women inmates. In response to those problems, Thyra Thomson, SBCR member and Wyoming's first woman secretary of state, suggested two courses of action. First, she suggested the SBCR consider "the possibility of an adjunct facility to another institution." And, second, she offered that "community-based centers could be [built] specifically for women to solve part of the problem." Although an architect attending that meeting cautioned that a separate institution for women "in the immediate coming years was really not [an] available option for the State," the subject resurfaced six months later at the SBCR's December 6 session. While meeting with a planning team to discuss a site for the new state penitentiary (south of Rawlins), the group also talked about the issue of women prisoners.

On January 3, 1977, Bruce Murray, Wyoming's Corrections Coordinator, told the SBCR that officials with the State of Nebraska Department of Correctional Services advised him that, after caring for 140 prisoners from the Cowboy State, they would "no longer accept Wyoming Women Felons after June 30, 1977. The Nebraska Center for Women can no longer accommodate the population from Wyoming in the area of housing and programming."

Responding to the state's problem of housing its own female felons, the SBCR returned such women to Wyoming and relocated them to the Wyoming State Hospital in Evanston. There, in July 1977, the SBCR officials designated Sheridan Hall, a converted adolescent unit near the front of the hospital's grounds, as the Wyoming Women's Center (WWC) and named Judy Uphoff the Facility Manager. She took delivery of the first inmates returning to Wyoming from Nebraska on Monday, July 11. Under her guidance there, a total of ninety prisoners eventually won their freedom from that facility.

As Wyoming's women prisoners increased in number, the state needed additional space in which to house them. So at the SBCR's October 5, 1979, meeting, Secretary of State Thomson recommended $287,272 be spent from Wyoming's Omnibus Land Income Fund to remodel not only Sheridan Hall, but Teton and Sweetwater Halls at the Wyoming State Hospital as well. The SBCR also recognized the inevitable: despite the obvious problems involved with financing a new women's institution, the state needed a permanent women's correctional facility based at a location other than at the Wyoming State Hospital. The Forty-Fifth State Legislature apparently anticipated that problem, because it instructed the SBCR to "recommend a site for the permanent location of the Wyoming Women's Center to the general session of the forty sixth Legislature."

Based on that directive, James B. Griffith, State Auditor and SBCR member, recommended at the SBCR's July 6, 1980, meeting that the Board proceed "on the same basis as was done with the new site [selection] for the new Wyoming Law Enforcement Academy," and a search began for towns interested in hosting such an institution.

Two months later (September 8), the following communities made presentations to the SBCR hoping to become the site for the new Wyoming Women's Center: Casper, Douglas, Glenrock, Lander, Lusk, Powell, Thermopolis, and Worland. Subsequent study, however, quickly culled the less appropriate sites as Donald G. Glidden, the SBCR's Executive Secretary, summarized in his findings:

> Lusk offered 70 acres of land at a cost of $1 per acre and that the site was especially desirable because it presented a variety of options for terrain on which the new facility could be built. Lander offered to donate land near the Training School; Thermopolis was found unsuitable because of its inner-city location and other land offered there would cost over one million dollars.

Powell offered a number of sites, including a WWII Internment Camp for Japanese [Heart Mountain] owned by the Federal Government, while Casper offered a number of sites found unsuitable because of their locations. Douglas offered the same land for the Women's facility as was offered for the [Wyoming Law Enforcement] academy. Worland had a number of acres for sale next to the Wyoming Industrial Institute and Glenrock had 50 acres for sale but close to a river.

WYOMING WOMEN'S CENTER

Given those options, State Auditor Griffith moved that Lusk be selected as the most desirable site. Governor Ed Herschler promptly seconded the motion, which carried without discussion. Following appropriate bidding, the State issued contracts on February 7, 1982, and construction of the new state-of-the-art "open penitentiary" began soon thereafter.

The resulting main building, of structural concrete block and brick veneer, encompassed 63,000 square feet on one level. It contained fifty medium-security cells, twenty maximum-security units, ten infirmary cells, a gymnasium, and mechanical area. The project also included a 3,400-square-foot pre-work-release building and a three-thousand-square-foot warden's residence, both of made of wood. Thirty-four cameras monitored the facility, and an elaborate alarm system and electronic locking mechanisms enhanced security.

Finally, on September 8, 1984, when Warden Uphoff with her staff and thirty-eight inmates entered the new facility at Lusk, Wyoming, authorities declared their new Women's Center to be officially open for business. Upon their arrival there on Tuesday, September 11, 1984, Uphoff said, "They were overwhelmed at the new facility and the size; it is quite an adjustment for them."

In 1996, due to overcrowding at the WWC, Wyoming authorities double-bunked the beds there so as to increase the institution's capacity from eighty-four to 144 women. The number of inmates confined to the building, however, continued to grow until only months before the second millennium arrived, 151 lived there full time. Due to lack of regular beds, they had to sleep in the infirmary or on "sled beds" on loan from the Wyoming State Penitentiary. To improve the care and control of those women, the Wyoming Department of Corrections (WDC) authorities studied a wide variety of options. As in the past, one of the most attractive involved the transfer of some inmates to other states. "We looked at Texas, but that wasn't appropriate" said Judy Uphoff, who had since been promoted to WDC's director. "There were beds in Virginia, but that was too far."

Finally, in August 1999, Wyoming's officials contracted at an inmate cost of $47.45 per day with the Central Oklahoma Correctional officials to transfer fifty of the Cowboy State's female inmates to a twenty-four-acre, medium-security facility in McLoud, Oklahoma. Housing the women in the Lusk facility cost the state twenty-one percent more, or $57.13 per inmate day. The contract, which extended to June 30, 2000, cost the State of Wyoming an additional sixty thousand dollars for the women's medical care, inmate incentive pay, and transportation expenses for prisoners and (WDC) Operations officials to monitor the women.

Of forty-six women thirty-three who volunteered and met the prescribed requirements, were transferred Thursday, September 9, some one thousand miles southeast to their new home in Oklahoma. Seventeen other inmates went involuntarily. Under (WDC) criteria, women who did not have major medical concerns or major behavioral problems were eligible for transport. Oklahoma statues exclude inmates convicted of capital crimes or sex offenses, those with escape histories, those who have participated in riots, and those classified as "maximum custody."

Thanks to this arrangement, the State of Wyoming not only benefits financially, but its inmates are offered enhanced programs to help them "build self-esteem, learn to be successful in the workplace, live peacefully with others, contribute positively to the community." Oklahoma, too, has gained from the relationship. The McLoud facility, according to Deputy Warden Jill Watson, which can accommodate a total of 850 inmates, only housed 679 there prior to this most recent agreement.

Since that first delivery of prisoners to the WWC in Lusk through the end of 1999, 758 women served time there. That brings the grand total to 1,100 Wyoming petticoat prisoners caught, convicted, and imprisoned in various state penal institutions for committing felonies since Molly Wrisinger gained the dubious distinction, 108 years ago, of becoming the state's first numbered woman inmate.

Given our human frailties and society's demand for retribution, there will regrettably be more. Many, many more.

SOURCES CITED

One of the most important primary documents that contributed to this epilogue—covering approximately seventy-four years—is a list of Wyoming women prisoners, beginning with Annie Bruce, Inmate #1, in 1908, through Joni Alberta Clementson, Inmate #273, in 1982. (Note: Authorities identified Annie Bruce as Inmate #1206, but she later was re-designated as Inmate #1 when they transferred her to the Colorado State Penitentiary.) The data includes each prisoner's name, identification number, location of imprisonment, age, birthplace, crime committed, county where offense took place, term of court, occupation, ethnicity, religion, habits of life, education, sentence date, term (length of imprisonment), term expiration date, maximum "good time," earliest discharge date, date of parole (if applicable), discharge date, and remarks.

Also on file at the Wyoming State Archives are the invaluable microfilmed (#1249) Board of Charities and Reform minutes for the period 1891-1961. The records that proved most helpful can be found in the following: Books D-F (March 9, 1903—June 29, 1910) and Books J-M (March 7, 1927—November 7, 1947), Books N-P (December 1, 1947—September 29, 1977), Book R (1970-1977), Book S (October 1977—April 5, 1982), and Book T (May 1982—October 1985). See, too, the "Governor's Message" in the Senate Journal of the Tenth State Legislature, 1909, p. 36, for that administration's interpretation of state law and its application to Wyoming's women prisoners during the first decade of the twentieth century.

The most contemporary sources of information about the handling of Wyoming's women prisoners during the past ninety years came via correspondence with correctional officials at institutions where they were incarcerated. These included letters from Mike Neve, Classification Administrator at the Lansing Correctional Facility in Lansing, KS (December 8, 1997); Larry Wayne, Warden at the Nebraska Correctional Center for Women in York, NE (December 1, 1997), and Susan Wigetman, Community Hospital Relations Coordinator at the Wyoming State Hospital in Evanston (December 3, 1997). Additional information was gained during telephone conversations with Acting Warden Nola Blackburn at the Wyoming Women's Center in Lusk, WY (December 1997-January 1998).

Perhaps the most helpful secondary sources are newspaper accounts in the *Uinta County Herald* (February-July 1977) and the *Lusk Herald* (September 6-20, 1984) about the handling of women prisoners after they were returned to Wyoming for confinement.

Also helpful were these articles: Tim Lockwood, "Female Inmates Move," *Wyoming Tribune-Eagle*, September 3, 1999, pp. A1, A6; also Tiffany Edwards, "Fifty Women Inmates Sent To Oklahoma," *Casper Star-Tribune*, Casper, WY, September 10, 1999, pp. B6, B2. Chris Thayer, Executive Assistant to WWC Warden Nola Blackburn, provided the updated statistics regarding women prisoners at Lusk.

Appendix

Female Felons Imprisoned at the Wyoming State Penitentiaries

NETTIE STEWART-WRIGHT

Crime/Location: Suspected of stealing government property, Buffalo
Entered Prison: Last week of July 1880
Released: Held nearly two weeks, but turned loose August 6, 1880, due to lack of evidence

FLORENCE W. HUGHES

Crime/Location: Suspected of selling liquor without a license, Cummins City
Entered Prison: June 1883
Released: Held three days; released due to lack of evidence

JENNIE BERRY

Crime/Location: Murder, accessory after the fact, twelve miles east of Fort Laramie on the North Platte River
Entered Prison: On or about June 13, 1887 and on March 6, 1888, she was transferred to Laramie County Jail in Cheyenne to serve the balance of her sentence
Pardoned: February 5, 1889

ANNA PETERSON

Crime/Location: Stealing cattle, Fremont County
Entered Prison: Entered Fremont County Jail November 11, 1887
Pardoned: November 10, 1888

INMATE #10: MARY WRISINGER

Crime/Location: Grand larceny, Laramie
Entered Prison: September 21, 1891
Term expired: March 15, 1893

INMATE #11: BELLE JONES

Crime/Location: Grand larceny, Laramie
Entered Prison: September 21, 1891
Term expired: March 15, 1893

INMATE #40: FLORENCE GAINES

Crime/Location: Assault with intent to kill, Cheyenne
Entered Prison: December 27, 1892
Term expired: November 6, 1893

INMATE #150: STELLA F. GATLIN

Crime/Location: Stealing articles of value from U.S. mails, Myersville
Entered Prison: November 28, 1893
Term expired: December 9, 1894

INMATE #259: CAROLINE WINFIELD
(same as Inmate #365, Caroline Hayes)

Crime/Location: Arson, Rock Springs
Entered Prison: May 13, 1896
Term expired: August 27, 1897

INMATE #271: MINNIE SNYDER

Crime/Location: Manslaughter, near Marquette
Entered Prison: July 9, 1896
Term expired: August 29, 1901

INMATE #280: ANNIE CURLEY JOHNSON

Crime/Location: Selling liquor at retail without first paying tax, Cheyenne

Entered Prison: July 23, 1896

Term expired: June 2, 1897

INMATE #365: CAROLINE HAYES
(same as Inmate #259, Caroline Winfield)

Crime/Location: Burglary, Laramie

Entered Prison: February 28, 1898

Term expired: November 17, 1899

INMATE #459: ELIZA STEWART

Crime/Location: Assault to commit manslaughter, Hanna

Entered Prison: November 14, 1899

Term expired: August 4, 1901

INMATE #510: LILLIE TODD

Crime/Location: Grand larceny, Cheyenne

Entered Prison: August 8, 1900

Term expired: July 2, 1901

INMATE #680: PEARL SMITH

Crime/Location: Entering store to commit felony, Rawlins

Entered Prison: June 4, 1902

Pardoned: December 17, 1902

INMATE #681: GERTIE MILLER

Crime/Location: Entering store to commit felony, Rawlins

Entered Prison: June 4, 1902

Pardoned: August 26, 1902

INMATE #780: EMMA L. NASH

Crime/Location: Forgery and counterfeiting, Rawlins
Entered Prison: October 13, 1903
Term expired: August 22, 1904

INMATE #817: VIOLA BIGGS

Crime/Location: Kidnaping, Casper
Entered Prison: March 24, 1904
Released on order of the Wyoming Supreme Court: August 25, 1904

INMATE #818: ANNA E. TROUT

Crime/Location: Kidnaping, Casper
Entered Prison: March 24, 1904
Released on order of the Wyoming Supreme Court: August 25, 1904

INMATE #965: HATTIE LAPIERRE

Crime/Location: Manslaughter, Thermopolis
Entered Prison: January 7, 1906
Pardoned: January 29, 1907

INMATE #1013: DOLLY BRADY

Crime/Location: Robbery, Cheyenne
Entered Prison: July 2, 1906
Term expired: March 26, 1908

INMATE #1080: GERTY BROWN

Crime/Location: Robbery, Cheyenne
Entered Prison: April 2, 1907
Term expired: February 29, 1908

INMATE #1148: ANNIE GROVES

Crime/Location: Felonious assault, Encampment
Entered Prison: October 17, 1907
Pardoned: February 9, 1908

INMATE #1206: ANNA FLORENCE BRUCE

Crime/Location: Manslaughter, Smoot
Entered Prison: April 17, 1908
Transferred to Colorado State Penitentiary: October 7, 1909
Pardoned: June 6, 1911

INMATE #1232: ELLA SMITH

Crime/Location: Misbranding livestock, Meeteetse
Entered Prison: June 6, 1908
Term expired: September 16, 1909

Index

Murphy, Joseph, 115-117, 119-121, 127-129
Murray, Bruce, 234
Myersville, WY, 40-45, 51

Nash, Emma Lenora, 131-136, 244
Nash, Jas., 132
Nash, Joseph F., 131-136
Nebraska Center for Women, 234
Nelson, Albert, 43
Nelson, Ann, xv
Neve, Mike, 240
Nichols, L., 43
Nichols, William, 71
North Platte River, xviii

Osterhout, Al, 207-208

Page, Annie, 185
Pagett, W.F., 185
Papworth, O.T., 204
Parmalee, Judge, 223
Passwater, James E., 189-191, 193-194
Peck, I.W., 86
Peralta, Peter T., 165
Perry, Julia, 230
Peterson, Anna, xix-xx, 241
Peterson, Chas H., 212
Peterson, Louis, 190
Peterson, Mrs. C.H., 212
Pierce, Sheriff, 218
Pierce, W.E., 69-72, 74
Pindell, Craig, xv, 254
Pleasants, Alice, 33-34
Pole Mountain, 26
Potter, Charles N., 154, 226
Powder River, 90
Powell, WY, 235-236

Preston, D.A., 165

Rankin, Joseph P., 43, 45, 50
Rawlins and Northwestern Stage Line, 39
Rawlins Mercantile Company, 119
Rawlins Republican, 104, 128, 137
Rawlins, WY, x, xiii, xiv, 40-41, 43, 100, 116-117, 120-121, 123-124, 127, 131, 134-136, 150, 165, 177, 183-184, 186-187, 193-194, 208-209, 217, 224-225, 227-228, 234
Reed, C.M., 230
Reed, R. Harvey, 98, 100
Reeves, Jack, 205
Reeves, Joseph, 205
Rice, Richard, xviii, xix
Richards, DeForest, 78-82, 124-128
Richards, James R., 157, 163-164
Richards, William A., 77-78, 82
Ridgley, H.S., 221-223
Riner, John A., 49, 87, 95, 218
Roach, A.S., 231
Robertson, O.J., 218
Rock Springs, WY, 57, 98, 119-120, 176
Roe, Richard, 56
Roedel's, A.E., 34
Rogers, C.J. "Doc," 232-233
Rooks, John, 70-74, 82
Ross, William B., 175, 179, 185
Rothwell, E.C., 233
Ryckman, J.H., 202-204, 206-207

Sanderson, Robert, xviii, xix
Schnitger, Gustave, xviii
Scholes, Constable, 183
Scott, Richard H., 34-35, 135

photo by Craig Pindell

ABOUT THE AUTHOR

LARRY K. BROWN, a fifth-generation published writer, earned a degree in journalism from the University of Nebraska in 1960 before entering the U.S. Air Force where he spent the next twenty years as an Information/Public Affairs officer. During his military career, he graduated from Boston University with a master of science degree in public relations and mass communications.

In 1980 he went to work for the Sun Company, Inc. and five years later was named Director, Public Relations and Communications for Sun Exploration and Production Company. In 1987 Brown joined the staff of the American Heart

Association (AHA) national headquarters, and the following year was sent to Wyoming as the Executive Director, AHA-Wyoming, Inc.

His writing credits include articles in such publications as *Wild West, True West, American Cowboy, Wyoming Magazine, Wyoming Annals,* and *Wyoming History Journal.* He also researched and scripted a two-hour *Today* show aired in 1979 by NBC-TV as well as a one-hour *Prime Time Sunday* program broadcast the following year by ABC-TV.

His *Hog Ranches of Wyoming: Liquor, Lust, and Lies Under Sagebrush Skies,* for which he received the "Western Horizon Award" from Wyoming Writers, Inc., was published in 1995 by High Plains Press. *You Are Respectfully Invited to Attend My Execution* (High Plains Press: 1997) was the second book of his Wyoming Frontier Crime Trilogy.

Brown is an active member of Western Writers of America and Wyoming Writers, Inc. He and his wife Florence, who make their home in Cheyenne, have four grown children.

*A special limited edition of 300 copies of this volume
was printed simultaneously with the trade paperback edition.
The special edition is Smyth sewn,
bound in Roxite B in Merlot Burgundy linen,
and stamped in coin gold foil.
It is designed to be sold without a dust jacket.*

*The text is composed in
twelve-point Adobe Garamond.
Display type is Post Antiqua BE with ornaments from Minion.
The book is printed on
sixty-pound Writers Offset B21 Natural
an acid-free paper
by Thomson-Shore.*